This volume provides essential information for people who experience rage and the mental health professionals who work with them. Potter-Efron's comprehensive and detailed descriptions of the nature and determinants of four different kinds of rage will also be of great interest to the general reader. The interpersonal and behavioral factors that trigger these overwhelming experiences of the extreme expression of anger are clarified, with excellent examples of the manifestation of rage. These recommendations for dealing with intense emotional experiences will help the reader to both understand and cope more effectively with rage-related problems.

> —Charles D. Spielberger, Ph.D., ABPP, distinguished research professor and director, of the Center for Research in Behavioral Medicine and Health Psychology at the University of South Florida in Tampa, FL

Finally a book that specifically deals with the many facets and complexities experienced in rage! Readers will be able to assess their own specific type of rage easily while also learning useful techniques for intervening and stopping such uncontrollable eruptions. This book is an excellent tool for individuals who are trying to gain more control over their emotions and counter the feelings of helplessness that often accompany experiences of rage. I highly recommend this book to anyone wanting to make significant changes in his or her life.

> —Kimberly Flemke, Ph.D., assistant professor in the Graduate Programs of Couples and Family Therapy at Drexel University in Philadelphia, PA

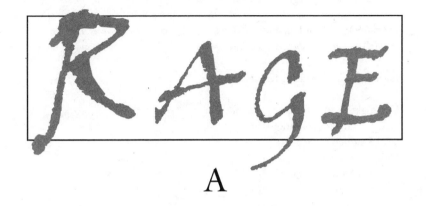

RAGE

A

Step-by-Step

Guide to

Overcoming

Explosive

Anger

RONALD T. POTTER-EFRON,
MSW, PH.D.

New Harbinger Publications, Inc.

Publisher's Note

Distributed in Canada by Raincoast Books

Copyright © 2007 by Ronald Potter-Efron
New Harbinger Publications, Inc.
5674 Shattuck Avenue
Oakland, CA 94609
www.newharbinger.com

Acquired by Catharine Sutker; Cover design by Amy Shoup;
Edited by Brady Kahn; Text design by Tracy Carlson

Library of Congress Cataloging-in-Publication Data

Potter-Efron, Ronald T.
  Rage : a step-by-step guide to overcoming explosive anger / Ronald T. Potter-Efron.
    p. cm.
  ISBN-13: 978-1-57224-462-7 (pbk.)
  ISBN-10: 1-57224-462-3 (pak.)
  1. Anger. I. Title.
BF575.A5P857 2007
152.4'7--dc22
                              2006102715

13 12 11

10 9 8 7 6

This book is dedicated to my wife, Patricia Potter-Efron, in deepest appreciation for her continuing support, help, and encouragement.

Contents

Acknowledgments

I first want to express my thanks to Brady Kahn, the editor of this book on rage, for her thoughtful and careful work. Also, my thanks to Matt McKay, Catharine Sutker, and the many professionals at New Harbinger Publications for continuing to support my writings in the area of anger.

Next, I thank several residents of a nearby boot camp who allowed me to interview them as they described their rages, near rages, and partial rages. Their openness helped me better understand the raging phenomenon.

Finally, I thank those people who read early versions of this book. Their comments helped me write more clearly and meaningfully. Readers included Charles Spielberger, Richard Pfeiffer, Pat Potter-Efron, Dave McQuarrie, Marie McDade, Rich Dowling, Linda Klitzke, and Alex Roseborough. Many of these people are connected with the National Anger Management Association in New York City or with First Things First Counseling in Eau Claire, Wisconsin.

What Is Rage?

Are You a Rager?

Something strange and scary happens to some people. On occasion, they lose control over their bodies, their brains, and their behavior. They say and do things that they later deeply regret. To illustrate, let me introduce you to four people who rage.

Lyle: A Victim of Child Abuse Still Fighting for His Life

Lyle almost died when he was only eight years old. His dad just about killed him. All he'd done was to forget to stack firewood for the woodstove. Dad came home, saw it wasn't done, and beat Lyle unconscious. His ma took him to the hospital. She lied, of course, about what happened. Told the doctors Lyle had fallen and smacked his head. Maybe they believed her. Maybe not. They patched him up. After that, Lyle never was the same. He got mean. He hated his dad. Finally, at age sixteen, Lyle was big enough to turn the tables. One night he went crazy. He doesn't remember what happened. His kid sister told him he started screaming at their father and then charged right at him. He knocked his dad down and kicked him. He beat the crap out of his father.

Here's the problem. Lyle's a thirty-year-old man now. But he can't control his emotions. He gets angry a lot. Really angry. And then he blacks out, just like that first time at age sixteen. Lyle's afraid he'll kill somebody one day. And he might—unless he gets some help soon.

Brenda: The Woman Whom Everybody Ignores

Brenda has always been the kind of person who blends into the background. Not very noticeable. Nice, but nothing special about her. Quiet. There she is now, smiling at her boss as he jokingly ignores all her good ideas. And, at the party, Brenda seems not to mind that her husband openly flirts with other women. Ah, but if people could only read her mind, they'd discover that Brenda's fuming inside. Maybe then they wouldn't be so surprised when she snaps, something she does about once a month. Man, you wouldn't believe the words that come out of that woman's mouth! It's like she isn't herself. Afterwards, Brenda always says she's sorry. She feels horrible about what she's said. But Brenda also says she can't control herself. It's like those words just roll off her tongue without her having any say in the matter. It's almost as if someone else, not Brenda, were speaking.

Ricardo: A Proud Man Too Easily Humiliated

Ricardo is a hard worker and a good provider. Unfortunately, though, he has very fragile self-esteem. He wants to believe he's a winner, but he's secretly afraid he's really a loser in life. That makes him very sensitive to criticism. So, the other day, when his boss told him that he had to redo some paperwork, Ricardo blew a fuse. "Who are you to tell me what to do, you fat old pig?" he yelled at his boss. He got so angry that two security men had to escort him out of the office. He lost his job that day, just as he'd lost several previous jobs. "I just can't take it when they put me down," he sobbed to his wife later that day. "I tell myself to stay calm, but I just can't. Something happens to me, and I go crazy."

Sharelle: A Woman Who Cannot Handle Abandonment

Here's Sharelle's story: "My boyfriend said he needed a little more space. He said we were getting too close. I went nuts. I threw a vase at his head." Sharelle gets so preoccupied with the men she falls in love with that she loses herself. She becomes really jealous, too. She better not catch her man so much as peeking at another woman, or all hell will break loose. But mostly, Sharelle is terrified of being abandoned. That probably goes back to when her mother died when Sharelle was only five years old. Her father disappeared from her life a couple years later. So when her boyfriend backs off even a little bit, Sharelle has an immediate meltdown. She cries uncontrollably. She shakes. Once she got so angry that she aimed a shotgun right at her boyfriend's heart. At least she thinks she did that. Her memory of events like this is pretty vague.

Lyle, Brenda, Ricardo, and Sharelle—and perhaps you, the reader, as well—all suffer from *rage*. This mysterious event can be defined as an experience of excessive anger accompanied by partial or complete loss of conscious awareness, a normal sense of self, and/or behavioral control. Each of these people becomes, for a little while, someone different from themselves. As one of my clients told me of how he'd jumped out of a car to pummel a man who had just insulted him, "Someone else got out of that car. It wasn't really me."

How Common Is Raging?

If you are a rager, you may believe you are the only person on this planet with that particular problem. Actually, you have plenty of company. In fact, author and psychiatrist John Ratey (Ratey and Johnson 1998), in reviewing the literature on rage, writes that "one in five normal, everyday people experiences violent attacks of rage that he or she cannot control" (149). Now this doesn't mean that 20 percent of the population gets homicidally mad on a regular basis. But, what it does mean is that many people do become so irate, from time to time, that they say and do things they later regret. Furthermore, these individuals often say that they don't like losing control that way but that, when it happens, they truly cannot stop themselves.

I am a clinical psychotherapist in Eau Claire, Wisconsin. Eau Claire is a rather sleepy city of only 60,000 people. It is family oriented, religious, and quiet. There are no real gangs in Eau Claire, Wisconsin—just a few wannabes. In other words, you would probably expect there to be precious few ragers in my humble burg. You would be wrong. My caseload is full of people who display both sudden and seething rages—short-fused screamers and long-term resenters. Abandonment rages are routine, since Eau Claire suffers from the same problem with failing relationships that is so common everywhere in the United States. Job layoffs have added to many workers' sense of impotent rage. Too many of the people in my town feel tremendous shame and sometimes react with great anger to the slightest insult. And, sadly, Eau Claire has its full share of men and women who have survived severe trauma, only to be left with a terrified, defensive stance toward life.

I believe Ratey's statistics. I agree that 20 percent of the population rages at least occasionally. That makes rage a significant problem in American society (and probably in many other countries as well).

A Closer Look at Rage

Let's break down the definition of rage into its component pieces:

An Experience of Excessive Anger

Too much anger! That's a big part of the rage experience. But what does that mean? When is too much too much? Here's one explanation. Imagine that every person alive carries around an emotional container. The job of that container is to be a place we can fill with our strong emotions, in this case anger. The container is more like a balloon, though, than a box. When you're not angry, the balloon contracts. When you get mad, it fills up. It expands enough so that you can be angry, sometimes very angry, but still be yourself. Furthermore, some fortunate people seem to have balloons that can expand easily. They can get angry without any difficulty. It's as if their emotional balloon can just keep on expanding forever. But most people can't do that. They can only get so angry, and then the balloon starts to get stretched awfully thin.

Besides, no balloon can expand forever. At some point, you reach your limit. Your emotional balloon is full. But what if you still have more anger? How much more emotion can you force into the balloon? At some point, sooner or later, that balloon is going to burst.

Here's another analogy. Imagine that it's been raining for days and days. Water is pouring into streams and rivers, threatening to flood the land. Only a single dam lies in the way. But can that dam hold back the flood? The answer, if all that water represents anger, is usually yes. You might have to open the spillways for a while (maybe by taking a time-out or by being appropriately assertive or by using other anger management tools), but the dam has been built to withstand a lot of pressure. It would take a once-in-a-century flood to burst through the dam.

The point at which your emotional balloon pops, or when the dam bursts, is what I mean by the phrase *excessive anger*. It's a state of emotional overload that triggers all kinds of changes, none of them good. The three most significant of these problematic changes are covered below.

Partial or Complete Loss of Conscious Awareness

Lyle says he doesn't remember what he says and does when he rages. That's a fairly common experience, although many ragers

remember part of what they said or did, usually up to a certain point (when their emotional balloon pops) and perhaps a little of what happens after that. These memories will usually be more emotional than intellectual, more vague than detailed.

Lyle is having a *rage blackout*. That balloon has popped, and the first thing affected is the more evolved parts of his brain, including the part responsible for active conscious memory.

Partial or Complete Loss of a Normal Sense of Self

Brenda felt almost like someone else had taken over her body. That's also a common raging experience. Even if you stay conscious, you don't feel at all normal. You have a Dr. Jekyll and Mr. Hyde experience in which a mean and furious person seems to take over your body. Sometimes the takeover is partial and short lasting. Sometimes it is complete and long lasting.

Partial or Complete Loss of Behavioral Control

The scariest part of a rage episode, at least for bystanders, is that ragers may appear to lose control over their actions. At worst, ragers can and do kill people while raging. They also destroy precious objects, both their own and others'. They say awful things as well, oftentimes things they would never say at other times. Again, and fortunately, this loss of control may be only partial and temporary. Some ragers tell me they sense an internal battle during these moments between a destructive, violent, furious self and their more sane and peaceful self.

Rage Is a Transformative Experience

Here's what all this means. Rages occur when you become angry enough at the world (or yourself) that you can no longer contain your anger through your usual channels. Discussion doesn't help. Arguing is useless. Exercise fails. It's too late to take a time-out. Your emotional balloon, the one you use to contain your anger, bursts. The dam breaks. You then become someone noticeably different, if only for a few seconds and perhaps only to yourself. You are transformed.

Technically, this experience is called a *dissociative event*. But I want mostly to avoid that term because it has become too closely associated with people who have permanent splits in their experience of self, so-called multiple personalities. I'm not saying these people don't exist, however. It's just that the rager's experience is a more temporary one. It is an emergency measure the brain uses when it is simply overwhelmed with anger. True, the balloon pops. But once the emergency ends, almost always within minutes or a few hours, your normal personality returns. "It's over, I'm not angry anymore. I can come back now" is the theme song of the rager.

I do use the term *dissociation* when someone has what is often called a *blind rage*. A blind rage occurs when you have an exceptionally long-lasting loss of awareness during which you say or do excessively violent things. You may appear to be perfectly alert (perhaps pacing around, yelling, making threatening remarks) during a blind rage. But you really aren't yourself at all. Later, you'll report that you don't remember most or all of what happened. It is as if you had a circuit breaker in your brain that breaks the connection between your actions and what you are aware of doing. Nobody knows exactly why this happens. The best current guess is that during times of extreme stress and perceived threat, the brain goes into survival mode. Its only job right then is to keep you alive, if necessary, by destroying everything in your path. The brain essentially decides, "This is no time to think. Just act. Fight. Kill if necessary."

Blind rages are the most potent kind of transformative experience that ragers may have. They are true dissociative experiences, similar to but not the same as epileptic seizures. Blind rages are related to the way highly traumatized individuals repress extremely threatening events in their lives, such as near-death experiences or sexual assaults.

Here is one other distinction. A blind rage is different from an alcoholic or a drug-induced blackout. Alcoholic blackouts aren't emotional events. They aren't caused by emotional overload. However, use of alcohol or other mood-altering chemicals does make some people more likely to have rage blackouts. That's why you should avoid these substances if you have a problem with rage.

Other Important Characteristics of Rage

Rages always involve an experience of excessive anger and a transformative experience marked by loss of normal awareness, a changed sense of self, and loss of behavioral control. But people also often talk about the following aspects of rage:

- Total rages are far more intense than very strong anger.

- Rages may develop quickly and without warning.

- Rages may develop more slowly and less spontaneously.

- Four kinds of threatening situations can trigger rage.

- A distorted sense of danger leads to exaggerated actions.

The next part of the chapter will cover these different aspects.

Total Rage

A total rage is an extreme event, more powerful than even the strongest types of normal anger. When you have a total rage, the word "anger" completely understates your experience. To say that ragers get angry is like saying a tornado is a bad storm. No, you aren't angry. You are absolutely furious about whatever is troubling you. Total rage is the cyclone of wrath, the level five hurricane of vengeance. Rages like this are a total body-and-mind event that transforms a person into a potentially lethal instrument of destruction. Your entire body can become consumed in a rage. Your heart starts pounding. Your hands turn into fists that pound on tables until they are bloodied. Your voice may rise an octave. Your legs shake. Some people literally see red because the rush of blood being pumped far too quickly and powerfully expands the capillaries in their eyes.

You may instinctively understand this idea. You know you can talk with an angry person, even someone who is irate. You can calm them down. You can reason at least a little with them. But you also know or sense that there is no talking with someone having a total rage.

When you rage, you are in a world of your own. No matter what others say, you either don't hear it at all or you completely distort the message. When you hear "please calm down," you interpret it as "you're trying to control me again, aren't you?" You hear "I love you" as "I hate you."

But then, several minutes or hours later, or the next day, you might feel terribly guilty and remorseful. "I don't know what came over me," you might say. "I'm so sorry. I didn't want to scare you. I didn't mean to hit you. I promise I won't do it again. Please forgive me."

Note that not all rages are total rages. It's possible to experience smaller and less terrifying rages. The topic of partial and near rages is covered later in this chapter. First, I want to talk about six different kinds of rage.

Sudden Rage

Dr. Jekyll and Mr. Hyde. Sudden transformation. Quickly changing from normal to scary. Dangerous. That's a classic rage. If you act this way, you are having a *sudden rage*, defined as a rapidly appearing, unplanned, and unanticipated transformative anger experience during which you lose partial or complete control over your feelings, thoughts, and actions.

Sudden rages are unplanned. That doesn't mean they always come completely out of the blue, however. You may receive warning signs, such as noticing bad feelings building up inside. You may sense that you are getting close to a meltdown. That can be very helpful, because then you can get away from others, take appropriate medications, exercise, relax, or just talk with someone who can help you ward off the potential rage. But frequently, there are no particular signs or warnings. Instead, something happens that may seem minor to observers but feels instantly intolerable to you. That's when you lose control. You begin yelling, threatening, intimidating, attacking. You zoom past normal anger as if it were on a Sunday drive and accelerate instantly to a 100 mile-per-hour fury. You cannot be calmed with soothing words, because you aren't able to listen to anybody. And you don't stop until your surge of energy is exhausted.

Sudden rages are the topic of chapter 3 in this book.

Seething Rage

Rages aren't always a reaction to an immediate situation. Sometimes they build more slowly in response to what you feel is a terribly unfair situation. These rages are like underground fires, smoldering below your full consciousness for years before they finally break through to the surface. The result is a *seething rage*, which can be defined as a long-term buildup of fury toward a specific individual or cluster of individuals that includes a sense of having been victimized, obsessive thoughts about the situation, moral outrage and hatred toward the offenders, personality changes, vengeful fantasies, and (sometimes) deliberately planned assaults upon targeted offenders. People who struggle with seething rages almost always have to deal with a tremendously strong sense that the offenders who have harmed them are morally bad, monstrous, and evil. Seething rages are described in much more detail in chapter 4.

What Triggers Rage

People don't rage just because they feel like raging (although some people may fake a rage to get what they want). Rages are far too uncomfortable, exhausting, and dangerous to play around with. Instead, rages are usually triggered by a negative experience that you interpret as dangerous to some important aspect of your being.

What kinds of dangers are likely to trigger a rage? The most immediate threat, of course, is to your physical existence; therefore, one kind of rage is designed to help you survive physically threatening situations. The best name for this kind of event is *survival rage*. But there are at least three other types of threats that can trigger rages. Perhaps you cannot stand situations in which you feel out of control of your own life, or powerless over important events (whether or not you will be laid off from work in the next round of company cutbacks, for example). *Impotent rage* is the name for rages associated with this sense of helpless fury. This is the rage of a man shaking his fist at the sky, demanding that God explain why his son has just died.

A third kind of threatening situation may occur when you feel embarrassed, criticized, or humiliated. Now, certainly nobody likes this experience. Who would? But you might react incredibly intensely to perceived put-downs, whether or not the other person intends to be insulting you. If so, you could have a *shame-based rage*, in which you flail away verbally and sometimes physically at the people you think are shaming you.

Finally, a fourth kind of potentially rage-producing threat occurs if you cannot endure feelings of loneliness, anxiety, and insecurity. For instance, you may desperately want your partner back, even though that person just told you he or she is in love with someone else. You call to talk about it, only to hear yourself screaming that he or she is a horrible jerk whom you hate and never want to see again. At that moment, you are having an *abandonment rage*.

Survival rage. Impotent rage. Shame-based rage. Abandonment rage. These four kinds of rages overlap because each in its own way involves your fighting for something that feels absolutely necessary. First comes physical safety. Then the need to feel you can make things happen in critical situations. Then comes the need to be respected within the community as a member in good standing. And the final critical need is to belong with people who love and nurture you. Although these four needs differ, they have a common thread: survival in an often-threatening world.

Six different kinds of rage have now been mentioned. Two kinds of rage depend on how fast they develop: sudden and seething rages. Four types of rages are reactions to specific kinds of threats: survival rage, impotent rage, shame-based rage, and abandonment rage. These six kinds of rages will be described in more detail, along with tips on minimizing their power, in separate chapters later in this book.

Rage and a Distorted Sense of Danger

Every tool in the great toolbox of life has value. That is true even for raging, under certain circumstances. Most immediately, raging could help you survive in life-threatening situations. If an enemy is running toward you with a knife, for example, it's not a really great time to think too much ("Hmmm, let me consider the options here. I could fight. I could run. I could…"). Wouldn't it be a lot better right then to be able to do something, anything, to get out of danger? Just shut down your mind for a few minutes and start fighting for your life?

Hopefully, though, you face few life-threatening situations, even if you rage frequently. But that doesn't seem to make sense. If you are raging, even though there is no immediate actual threat to your existence—and rages only occur because people feel deeply threatened—what's going on? The answer, of course, is that you regularly feel deeply threatened, even when there is no real danger. You have a distorted sense of danger. You constantly feel attacked. The world, for you, is by no means safe and secure. Instead, you live in a place full of hostile, dangerous, and threatening adversaries.

How did you become convinced that you are in constant danger? Perhaps, at one time in your life, you really were seriously threatened or attacked. Or possibly, you did not have that kind of experience, but you grew up with parents who promoted the idea that the world is full of bad people. You may have suffered subtle damage to the brain, making it easy for you to misinterpret other people's intentions.

This sense of immediate danger can take over your mind during a rage episode. It's useless at those times to suggest that you should "just relax and don't let it bother you." You can't relax. You probably would if you could, but you can't. Your anger is feeding on itself by then. Anything someone else says just makes you angrier (especially the line "just calm down and get control of yourself"). You could almost say that at this point, you have become your rage and your rage has become you. By this time, your thoughts have become terribly distorted. All you can see around you are enemies ready to strike. You've got to defend yourself. Right at the moment of rage, you believe you must fight for your life in a totally hostile world. Your brain has only one job: find the danger, so it can be eliminated.

That brings you to actions. Chances are you don't live by the motto "all things in moderation" when you are raging. Probably your motto at those times would be more like "all things to excess." So you take sudden and impulsive actions. You make incredibly nasty verbal attacks. You may even become dangerously violent. And, true to the idea of transformation, you say and do things that you would never do if you weren't raging. Later, you might totally want to deny you did those things. But you did indeed do them, and now you'll need to take responsibility for your actions.

Partial Rages and Near Rages

Fortunately, not all rages are total rages. Most often, people only partially lose control of themselves during a rage. For instance, a former client named Herm reported that he got into a fight with another guy, went into a rage, and beat his opponent to the ground. But then Herm stopped himself, "just before I was gonna kick him in the head." Many other times, people rage verbally but don't become physical. They manage to contain themselves even though they "wanted to strangle him until his eyes bulged." This kind of episode is a *partial rage*, for you maintain some control over what is occurring even while the rage is happening. During a partial rage, you may attack verbally rather than physically, bypass one person to attack another, assault objects rather than people, or stop attacking even after starting. As for transformation, when you are having a partial rage, you may feel torn between your normal self and your raging self. Finally, your normal self regains control, and you settle down, probably angry but no longer raging.

You may remember times when you stopped yourself before you even began a rage episode. At those times, you were having a *near-rage* experience, in which you got close to having a rage and then somehow managed to stop it in its tracks. Allie, a middle-aged home-maker, for example, caught herself rapidly building up to a rage after her boyfriend came home drunk one night: "He had passed out on the floor, and there I was ordering him to get his ass upstairs into bed. He couldn't even hear me. I wanted so bad to kick him and hit him. I could feel myself losing it. But then I stopped. I don't know how, but I stopped. I just left him there on the floor and went to bed."

Partial rages and near rages represent the fuzzy middle ground between strong anger and total rages. They indicate that, at least some of the time, you have some control over your rages. That's good. It means that you can benefit from such standard anger management tools as taking time-outs and replacing your angry thoughts with calming thoughts. These tools will help you gain better control over your tendency to rage and supply you with better ways to handle difficult situations.

The High Cost of Raging

Here's one man's story: "I lost it. I had a total meltdown. First I started screaming at my wife to shut her damn mouth. Then I knocked over the table with all her important stuff on it. Then I slapped her face. That's when my kid called 911. Now I've got a restraining order against me. I can't even talk with my wife. I hope she'll take me back, but who knows? Man, why did I do such a stupid thing?"

Raging, especially sudden raging, doesn't come cheap. In fact, raging is a luxury few people can afford. Here are just a few of the costs of losing control of anger. How familiar are they to you?

Loss of freedom.   Jail, restraining orders, court-ordered anger management or domestic-abuse programs. These are common outcomes for ragers.

Physical damage to others.   Harming others, even the people you love and wish to protect. Later you'll feel awfully guilty, but the damage has already been done.

Fractured relationships.   Marriages, friendships, family ties. Who wants to hang around a loose cannon?

Broken promises to yourself.   You swear you'll never hurt someone like that again, only to have yet another blowup.

Getting fired, suspended, expelled.   People who rage at work or school frequently end up with a lot of time on their hands.

Financial stress.   Replacing broken objects. Incurring legal fees because of the trouble you get into during rages. Lost wages.

Others' fear and loss of trust.   Ragers have to contend with other people's fear of them as well as lost trust. It feels bad to realize that you have little or no credibility with the important people in your life because of these incidents. It's no fun to recognize that your children are so scared of you that they hide in their rooms when you come home.

Obsession, paranoia, and isolation.   Seething ragers often become more and more distrustful of others over time. You think constantly about your injuries and the people who harmed you. You may gradually become more and more paranoid, thinking that just about everybody is out to get you. You break off contact with others, which only gives you more time to obsess.

Self-hatred.   It's difficult to feel good about yourself when you have lost control of your emotions and damaged the people you love. It's not uncommon for ragers to punish themselves by turning their rage onto themselves, perhaps by scratching their face or driving their heads into a wall. They may even entertain thoughts of suicide as they face their shame and guilt after a rage episode.

Your life, if you are a rager, is probably difficult, painful, harsh, and lonely. Periodic losses of control disrupt the entire fabric of life, creating chaos at the center of your being. Nobody, not even you, knows what to expect. Who can say when you will disintegrate into fury again? What will happen then? What objects will get smashed? Whose body will be damaged? Which friend or lover will go away, perhaps never to return?

This just cannot go on. The rewards are too few, the costs so high. Something must change and change quickly. Fortunately, there are methods that you can use to quit raging. If you want to begin working on stopping your raging thoughts, feelings, and actions, this book can help you.

Now comes the moment of truth. Are you one of that 20 percent of the population with a rage problem?

What Comes Next

You may be reading this book just out of general interest. You may know or live with someone who is a rager. Or perhaps you're wondering if you may be a rager yourself. If the last is your concern, please take the questionnaire below. Your answers will help you decide if you do have a rage problem and, if so, what kinds of rages you have.

Rage Questionnaire

Instructions: For each of the statements below, give the answer that best describes you.

Y   "Yes, that's true about me at least once in a while."

N   "No, I'm sure that I don't do that or think like that."

M   "Maybe. I'm just not sure if that statement describes what I think or do."

*   "Yes, and very important. This is serious, dangerous, scary."

Sudden Rage Indicators

1. *My anger comes on both very quickly and very intensely.* _____

2. *I get so angry that I lose control over what I say or do.* _____

3. *People say I act strange, scary, or crazy when I get really mad.* _____

4. *I have blacked out (not from alcohol or drugs) when I became very angry so that I did not remember things I said or did.* _____

5. *I get so angry that I worry I might seriously harm or kill someone.* _____

6. *I feel like I become a different person when I get angry, as if I am not really myself.* _____

7. *I become instantly furious when I feel that somebody has insulted or threatened me.* _____

Number of items marked Y or * on 1–7: _____

Seething Rage Indicators

8. *I am unable to quit thinking about past insults or injuries.* _____

9. *My anger about some past insult sometimes seems to grow greater over time instead of leveling off or diminishing.* _____

10. *I sometimes have intense fantasies of revenge against people who have harmed me.* _____

11. *I hate people for what they have done to me.* _____

12. *People would be amazed if they knew how angry I get even though I don't show it.* _____

13. *I feel outraged about what people try to get away with.* _____

14. *I have difficulty forgiving people.* _____

15. *I seethe in anger but don't say anything to others.* _____

16. *I deliberately hurt people (physically or verbally) in order to pay them back for something they did to me.* _____

Number of items marked Y or * on 8–16: _____

Survival Rage Indicators

17. *I have gotten into a physical fight where it took several people to pull me away from the other person.* _____

18. *I threaten to severely hurt or even to kill people when I become very angry.* _____

19. *I startle easily in situations, such as when somebody touches me on the shoulder from behind.* _____

20. *I feel like I am fighting for my life when I become angry.* _____

21. *I go into a blind rage when defending myself against real or imagined danger.* _____

22. *People say I am paranoid or that I falsely believe that people are trying to harm me.* _____

23. *I have a fight-or-flight reaction, during which I feel both really angry and really scared.* _____

Number of items marked Y or ∗ on 17–23: _____

Impotent Rage Indicators

24. *I feel like exploding when people don't listen to me or understand me.* _____

25. *I blow up after thinking such thoughts as "I just can't take it anymore."* _____

26. *I feel both helpless and furious about situations I cannot control.* _____

27. *I pound the ground, break things, or scream out loud when things don't go the way I want them to.* _____

28. *I get so angry I have to do something—anything —even if it makes the problem worse.* _____

29. *I harbor thoughts of violence or revenge toward people who have (or once had) power or control over me.* _____

Number of items marked Y or ∗ on 24–29: _____

Shame-Based Rage Indicators

30. I become furious when people seem to disrespect me. _____

31. My reputation—my good name—is something I strongly defend. _____

32. I frequently worry that people think I am stupid, ugly, or incompetent. _____

33. I get really mad after a moment of embarrassment—for instance, if someone points out something I did wrong. _____

34. People say that I am way too sensitive to criticism. _____

35. I dwell upon put-downs that I believe people have made about me. _____

36. I become irate when people seem to be ignoring me. _____

Number of items marked Y or ∗ on 30–36: _____

Abandonment Rage Indicators

37. I become furious when I think about times when I have been abandoned or betrayed. _____

38. I struggle with intense feelings of jealousy. _____

39. I look for proof that the people who say they care about me cannot be trusted. _____

40. Feeling neglected or ignored by the people I love seems almost intolerable to me. _____

41. *I become preoccupied with wanting to get back at my parents or partners because they left me, neglected me, or betrayed me.* _____

42. *I feel cheated by my partner, children, or friends because I give them way more love, caring, and attention than I get back.* _____

43. *I have been told that once I become really mad, I can't take in any reassurances or statements of caring from the people I am angry with.* _____

Number of items marked Y or * on 37–43: _____

Interpretation. There is no minimum score on this questionnaire that says you have a rage problem. Instead, even one "yes" or "*" answer means you could have a problem with rage. The more "yes" or "*" answers in general, the more likely it is that you have a serious rage problem. The more "yes" or "*" answers in any single section, the more likely you have that kind of rage problem.

Now that you have completed the questionnaire, please use the rest of the space on this page to answer these two questions: Do you think you have a problem with rage? Why?

What Can You Do About Your Raging?

Raging is a serious problem. If your answers to the questionnaire indicate that you have a rage problem, then you need to do something about it fast. You can start by reading the remainder of this book, paying the most attention to the chapters that focus on your specific types of rage. But first, you probably want to think about what makes a person become a rager. That's the topic of the next chapter.

What Causes Rage?

The Origins of Rage

If you have problems with rage, you almost certainly ask yourself these questions: "Why am I this way? What makes me different from other people who never rage? Was I born this way? Do I rage because of things that happened as I was growing up?" These are very important questions to ask, because if you could get the answers, you would be better able to quit raging. The issue is complicated, however. That's because there is no single cause of rage. Instead, there are many possible contributors to the problem, each of which might be important for one rager but irrelevant to another. Some of the most general causes of rage will be described in this chapter. These include brain imperfections, emotional trauma, drug abuse, parental modeling, payoffs for raging, getting high by raging, and excessive experiences of shame and abandonment.

First, though, let me provide some background information for rage control by describing normal childhood and adolescent development.

Tantrums and Rage

Here's a point that will seem obvious to any parent: children and teenagers generally have more difficulty controlling their anger than adults. Why? Mostly because the parts of our brains that help us contain angry impulses develop slowly, for as long as twenty-five years, after we're born. In particular, the prefrontal lobes, nearest the forehead, help us delay hostile urges, figure out alternatives to exploding, and think in moral terms about the feelings and rights of others. So the average child simply cannot avoid the occasional tantrum, while the typical teen goes huffing and puffing to his or her room, screaming about stupid idiot parents who just don't understand and aren't being fair.

Not every child and adolescent rages, however. A rage is not the same beast as a tantrum. A kid having a tantrum has a goal. A kid having a rage is bent on destruction.

Nevertheless, most children do gradually get better and better at staying in control of their anger as they mature. However, some children have a harder time than others. These children seem to have been prone to anger since birth. They are easily upset and agitated when stressed.

Jimmy is an example of a child who has always had trouble controlling his extreme anger. Jimmy was ten years old when he came to therapy. Near the end of one therapy session, Jimmy asked his father if they could stop on the way home for a hamburger. His dad replied that stopping for a hamburger would not be possible, because he had to hurry home for a meeting. Instantly, Jimmy flew into a rage. He was shaking, screaming, crying, threatening to kill Dad and himself, not making sense, and totally unable to stop. At that moment, his father could have offered Jimmy a dozen burgers, and it would have done no good. He was in another world. All anyone could do was to keep Jimmy (and those around him) safe until the rage ran its course in about twenty-five minutes. Later, Jimmy did not remember what happened.

An example of an adolescent rager would be Jeff, a fourteen-year-old boy who only experienced rages at home, perhaps because there he could "relax" and quit trying to look good for his peers. Jeff's rages would always begin with a feeling of being overcome by a combination of shaky anxiety and numbing depression. That would last about fifteen minutes to an hour, and then he would explode, inevitably breaking both his own and his family's property. If his parents tried to stop him, things only got worse. But eventually the rage would die down, and he would then need to sleep for several hours.

Perhaps the best descriptions of childhood rages come from two well-known books written in the late 1990s. The first is *The Explosive Child*, by Ross Green (1998). The second is *The Bipolar Child*, by Demitri and Janice Papalos (1999). Green describes explosive children as relatively inflexible and unable to adapt to new situations, with extremely low tolerance for frustration, deficiencies in social skills, and high degrees of anxiety and irritability. These children often have difficulty thinking ahead and understanding issues. They also struggle with sensory integration, so that it is hard for them to combine different sensory data into one meaningful package. The frequent result of this combination of problems is a meltdown, a period of incoherent rage such as Jimmy displayed.

The Papaloses describe childhood rages among bipolar children, which are often triggered by a parent's limit-setting efforts. A simple "no" can set off an almost seizure-like episode in which the child may bite, hit, kick, break things, and scream foul language. They give examples of children who rage like this several times a day, for as long as three hours at a time.

Clearly, explosive children and bipolar children are different from "normal" children in their ability to handle frustration. You might be wondering if some or all of their problems could be caused by brain abnormalities. The Papaloses think this might be the case. They discuss how parts of the emotional control center of the brain, called the limbic system, may be damaged in these children. If so, that damage would help explain why these children cannot calm down and why they fly off the handle at any apparently minor frustration.

Brain damage and limitations may also be a major reason some adults rage. That topic is next on the agenda. But first, please think about these questions: How much do you know about your childhood rage history? Did you have meltdowns like the ones described above? How often? How serious were they? What did you, your parents, or professionals do to try to help you contain your rages?

Rages and Our Imperfect Brains

Joe is wonderful with numbers but has a lousy memory. Jorge has an artistic eye but can't put his ideas into words. Tatiana has instinctive social skills but poor reasoning ability. They all have less-than-perfect brains. So do the rest of us. Nobody's brain works well all the time in every situation. Each of us has a few weak spots where somehow our brain circuitry did not get constructed quite right.

Unfortunately, some people's brains are wired poorly in places where the control of emotion takes place. Their less-than-perfect brains may be the result of hereditary factors, illness or disease, physical injury, or even trauma. Whatever the cause, their relatively poor emotional control makes these individuals more likely to have rage attacks.

Emotions are really quite complicated things. We have emotions because we need them. Emotions act as messengers delivering vital information that we need to act upon. "Hey, that feels great. Keep doing it," says the messenger of joy. "I miss him so. Can't you get him back?" asks the messenger of sadness. And here comes the messenger of anger: "That stinks! I don't like it. Make them stop!"

A good brain does several emotional jobs. First, it creates electrical and chemical pathways that produce emotional responses. That means the brain has to make the messengers and send them on their way. Next the brain lets us interpret the messages (as in "I'm feeling really anxious right now"). Then, the brain has to inhibit the message so that it doesn't keep running on forever or build up too strongly. That's like telling the messenger, "Okay, thank you. I've got the message. You can go now."

All this is complicated. Furthermore, there is no single area of the brain that is solely responsible for emotional regulation. True, the limbic system (which includes the amygdala, septum, cingulate gyrus, and hippocampus) has been identified as being very involved with emotions and may be considered the brain's emotional center. But many other parts of the brain—including, for instance, the prefrontal lobes, the temporal lobes, the periaqueductal gray area, the basal ganglia, and the cerebellum—also are part of the emotional team. That means that many parts of your brain must be working well if you are to control your emotions instead of having them control you. It also means that if any of several parts of your brain are broken, poorly developed, or missing, you will have great difficulty controlling your feelings.

Here is one important example. At any time, the brains of approximately 10 percent of the population appear to produce too little serotonin, a neurotransmitter that helps transmit information across the tiny gaps between neurons in the brain. People with serotonin deficiency become sad, usually lack energy, and feel hopeless. They are often diagnosed with major depressive disorder. But serotonin does more than just help someone feel alive and energetic. It also helps with impulse control. So, many depressive individuals are prone to sudden bouts of anger. They might direct this anger outwardly, sometimes bursting into irrational rages. Or they could become suicidal, directing their anger inwardly against themselves.

Meanwhile, another neurotransmitter, dopamine, can trigger rages when people have too much, rather than too little, of it in their brains. One reason cocaine and methamphetamine users can become so violent is that these drugs raise the level of dopamine in the brain.

Hormone imbalances can also affect your ability to control anger and aggression. As you might expect, males with relatively high levels of testosterone have been shown to be slightly more prone to aggression than other males. But recent research indicates that estrogen may also play a role in both male and female aggression. What is particularly interesting here is that these two hormones both seem to magnify and distort people's perception of threat. And if you mistakenly think someone is being mean to you on purpose, then you are likely to counterattack with anger, aggression, and even rage. Hormonal changes in some premenstrual women are severe enough to make these women more vulnerable to rage episodes than they would normally be. Many female clients have informed me that they have anger problems three weeks out of every month, but it is only when they are premenstrual that they rage.

The Raging Brain

Daniel Amen is a researcher who has studied the brain extensively, using a special technique nicknamed SPECT (which stands for "single positron emission computed tomography") to study blood flow in the brain. The idea is that blood flows to the parts of the brain that are most active during the performance of any particular task. By comparing the pictures of many different people doing the same task, Dr. Amen can tell for any single person if some part of his or her brain is not active enough, just right, or too active. In *Firestorms in the Brain*, Amen (1998) describes three brain disturbances that are quite commonly found in ragers.

First, ragers often have decreased activity in the prefrontal cortex when they attempt to concentrate. This condition is often associated with attention-deficit disorder (ADD), but, of course, not everybody with ADD rages, and not all ragers have ADD. Decreased activity in the prefrontal cortex may mean that some people can have difficulty focusing and solving problems when something goes wrong and also have less ability to control their impulses.

Secondly, while the problem with the prefrontal lobes is under-activity, there is another part of the brain in which overactivity is associated with raging. Increased activity in the *anterior cingulate gyrus*, a portion of the brain that lies directly above the *corpus callosum* (the part of the brain that connects the right and left hemispheres), indicates that the cingulate is working too hard. People with this brain imperfection often get stuck in negative thought patterns. They can't let go of problems. They tend to obsess. When you can't let go of something bad, it often gets worse in your mind. Then it becomes intolerable, something you must fight. So, for instance, Dad tells his son to take out the garbage, and his son mutters the usual stuff under his breath as he obeys. Now any dad would get annoyed at his son's minor exhibit of surliness, but most fathers would shrug and chalk it up to typical adolescent nonsense. However, a man with an overactive anterior cingulate gyrus might not be able to stop thinking about that insult, letting it build for hours or days. A seething rage develops. Finally, that father might fly into a visible rage, charging into his son's room and demanding an apology for an incident his son has long forgotten. That's when Mom jumps in, trying to calm Dad down, only to have him turn to bitterly accuse her of always siding with their son.

The third rage-related brain problem Dr. Amen describes is abnormal (either too much or too little) activity in the *left temporal lobe*, a large structure on the left side of the head. Abnormal activity here leads to people having a quick temper. People with abnormal temporal lobe activity often report that they become really angry really quickly—a perfect formula for raging.

What would happen if you were unlucky enough to have all three of these problems, as some people do? Say your friend forgets to pick you up to head over to a party one night. Finally, you go in your own car. On the way there, you start thinking about this insult, and thinking, and thinking. You can't come up with a game plan, though, because as much as you are trying to stay calm, you are getting too angry to concentrate. Also, you can't calm down because all you can think about is how insulted you feel. So when you get there, you rush up to your friend and say the first thing that pops into your head: "You stupid jerk. I oughta kill you." And that immediately leads to a fistfight with your friend.

This seems like a good time to mention that some people with raging brains do benefit from taking prescription medicine. There are some excellent medications for people whose brains don't work quite right in the area of emotional regulation. For instance, Ritalin-like psychostimulants help increase prefrontal lobe activity, so people can concentrate and problem-solve better; antidepressants often decrease obsessive negative thinking; and anticonvulsant medications such as

Tegretol, Depakote, and Lamictal may help lengthen the all-too-short fuse of people with temporal lobe abnormalities.

If you are a frequent rager, you should at least consider taking medication. This is most true if you have tried seriously and repeatedly to control these episodes and have been unsuccessful. It is also critical that you think about medications if you become so rageful that you may harm others or yourself. The bottom line is that rages are dangerous events that must be stopped. If you can't stop them by yourself, even with the help of family, friends, religious figures, or trained therapists, then you need to put aside your ego and seek medical help. Make sure, when you do, that you speak with a well-trained psychologist, psychiatrist, or anger management specialist with whom you can describe your specific rage pattern.

There is one more brain problem that must be mentioned in any discussion of rage. That is the damage associated with emotional trauma. The next section discusses how this kind of brain problem may be a reaction to overwhelming stress.

Overwhelming Stress and Emotional Trauma

Stress can be defined as a bodily response to any physical, mental, or emotional strain or tension. Researchers have long known that moderate stress energizes people. How much would anybody get done without a little pressure to get that paper written on time, bring home the paycheck, or resolve that recent argument with your spouse? However, people do poorly when they have too much stress in their lives.

Here's a question for you. How well would you hold it together if, in just a few months time, all these things happened to you: your back went out so that you felt excruciating pain running down your legs; your child got really sick and was bedridden for weeks; your hours at your job got cut back, so you didn't have enough money to pay your bills; your best friend, the only person you could talk to, moved to another city; and your partner told you that he or she was thinking seriously about leaving you?

That's a lot of stress. Now, you might be one of the gifted few who could sail smoothly through these rough waters. Or, you might be one of the many who could barely keep your boat from sinking with all those things going wrong. And in that case, you might be feeling hopeless and depressed. Perhaps, you'd be so anxious you could not sleep. You might isolate yourself, just trying to get away from everybody and everything. Your body and mind might feel numb. You probably would be fighting off mental and physical exhaustion. You would be worrying, worrying, worrying. A sickening feeling of panic might creep over you. And you might be ready to rage.

Certainly not everybody becomes rageful under stressful conditions. But some people do. These are usually individuals who already tend to get angry a lot. They may have the ability to control their anger under normal circumstances. But they have a limited ability to handle stress without getting mad. If you are one of these people and are facing the level of stress just described, you are vulnerable to rage.

So, now imagine you are driving home after a particularly hard day. Sure enough, that idiot in the red convertible carelessly cuts you off, just as you are about to change lanes. That's something you hate, rude people who don't obey the rules of the road. A minute later, you get stuck in a traffic jam, and now you're barely moving forward. Guess who is right in front of you? Yep, that guy in the convertible, looking cool and relaxed. And suddenly you can't take it anymore. You start honking your horn and yelling at him. You rant. You scream insults at him and shake your fist. You challenge him to get out of his car and fight. There you are, sitting in your car, raging. You better hope that the guy in the convertible has a lot better ability to contain his anger right now than you do. If not, one of you could die.

The past can be another source of rage-inducing stress. This occurs when people have been subjected to terrible, life-threatening events in childhood, adolescence, or earlier adulthood. Trauma can actually produce brain injury that lessens your ability to control your emotions and may lead to rage attacks. Severe emotional trauma, the type that accompanies life-threatening situations—such as, if you are a victim of physical assault or rape, or if you are a witness to violence—frequently produces permanent changes in the brain. These changes are designed to help trauma survivors stay safe in a dangerous world. To do so, they become hyperalert to any signs of danger. They may also become hyperreactive to perceived danger. The unfortunate result is someone who first mistakenly thinks he or she is under attack and then mistakenly defends him- or herself against the attack. Trauma-related brain injury will be covered in much greater detail in chapter 5.

The question here, for you, is this: how closely connected are your rages to times of great stress? If your answer is "a lot," then you will need to do everything you can to learn good ways to manage or lessen your stress.

Alcohol, Drug Abuse, and Prescribed Medications

A nineteen-year-old college freshman named Jake was suspended from school after a very strange incident that occurred one Monday morning. He had been out drinking and drugging for the entire weekend. That Saturday and Sunday, he had consumed a combination of drugs—alcohol, painkillers, amphetamines, and "a few little green pills. I don't know what was in them." Jake had not drunk or used heavily in high school. But now that he was free from mom and dad's rules, he had been cutting loose. Unfortunately, Jake sometimes became violent when he drank or used drugs. In fact, just the weekend before, a couple of his friends had to pull him away before he got into a barroom brawl with another guy.

By Monday morning, Jake was withdrawing from a combination of at least four mind- and mood-altering substances. That's when Howie, his roommate, shook Jake to wake him up. Jake went crazy: "I don't really remember what happened. All I know is that I started punching Howie. I couldn't stop. I guess I grabbed him around the neck and tried to strangle him. And he's my best friend." Howie was taken to the hospital with serious injuries. Jake was suspended from college and faced the possibility of doing a year or more of jail time.

Jake's situation is obvious. He drinks, he uses drugs, he becomes violent. Maybe not each and every time, but often enough to establish a definite pattern. Jake is a "keep the plug in the jug" kind of guy.

He will need to stay alcohol and drug free the rest of his life to avoid raging.

If only it were that simple all the time. But it's not. Actually, the relationship between substance abuse and violence (including raging) is complicated. Here are a few of the possibilities. Use of alcohol or mood-altering chemicals may do the following:

■ Disinhibit your underlying anger so that you may say, "Now I can tell you how I really feel, you stupid..." Perhaps you are already angry before getting high. But taking the substance turns potential aggression into the real thing. Note, though, you may expect this to happen. You might even want it to happen. That means your aggression may really occur not so much from the immediate effects of the drug but from your belief that you will become angry once you get loaded.

■ Promote irritability while you're intoxicated. This is a "don't mess with me when I'm drunk" situation.

■ Increase the likelihood for raging during withdrawal from the substance. That's Jake's situation.

■ Produce a long-term personality change associated with brain damage that increases the risk for raging. For example, if you use too many amphetamines (speed; meth) you could become so irrational that you end up being labeled as paranoid or paranoid schizophrenic.

■ Help you stuff your anger instead of talking about it. Marijuana users, for instance, sometimes claim that they become more mellow when stoned. However, the research does not back up that claim. In fact, some people become more, not less, angry on marijuana, so be cautious about trying to use marijuana to calm down.

Here is the worst-case scenario. Missy is someone who already has a history of strong anger and aggression. She knows that getting high only increases the possibility for violence. But that's okay. Missy likes to take risks. Besides, she can't feel good unless there is a lot of action going on. Getting angry, getting high—they both help Missy feel alive and energetic. So off she goes, heading to the tavern with every intention of drinking until she can't stand up, snorting a few lines of cocaine in the restroom, gulping down some pills. But something strange happens this evening. Somehow Missy feels higher than she ever gets. And then she becomes angrier than she has ever felt. The combination of drugs and anger has produced what is called a *synergistic effect*. It turns out that mixing booze and drugs with anger has multiplied the effects of both. So Missy becomes a human nuclear bomb. She flies into a total rage, throwing her glass, breaking her pool stick, swearing a blue streak, challenging everyone, male or female, to fight, until, finally, she gets thrown out of the place at one in the morning with nowhere to go and no way home.

If you have a problem with rage, then you must be completely honest with yourself about your use of mood-altering substances. Frankly, they may be a luxury you cannot afford.

So far, this section has discussed how alcohol and drugs might relate to rage. But there is something else to think about as well, namely that it is possible (although rare) for ordinary people to develop rage problems when they are taking prescribed medications exactly as directed. Have you ever heard of the term "iatrogenic effect"? It's an important term to know if you take any prescription medications. An *iatrogenic effect* is something unexpected and unfortunate that happens after someone takes a medication, even when that individual takes it exactly as prescribed. Examples would include breaking out in a rash, getting splitting headaches, fainting, and so on.

Suddenly becoming rage-prone is one very dangerous iatrogenic effect that does happen from time to time. In particular, rage reactions are not uncommon when physicians prescribe benzodiazepines, such as Valium, even though those medications are meant to help people calm down. However, the issue is not about controlling this one group of medicines; the problem is more random than that. The fact is that, although it's highly unlikely, any person could become unable to control anger and aggression with many prescribed medications. That means you should always monitor the effects of the medications you and your loved ones take. If you do notice an increase in anger, aggression, or rage that began about the time someone started a medication, you should contact the prescribing physician immediately.

This warning is especially apt for two groups. Please check to see if you belong to either one. The first group, as you might expect, is made up of people who already have problems with anger, aggression, and rage. They're already so close to melting down that even a little extra agitation, energy, or disorientation may shove them over the edge. The second group consists of recovering alcoholics and addicts, many of whom have very powerful and unpredictable reactions to medications. If you are in either group, you should be extra careful when beginning a new medication and keep careful records of any medications that have increased your anger or lessened your ability to control your impulses.

Rage Training in Childhood and Rage Rewards

We humans usually obey two simple rules: do what our parents do and do what gets rewarded. These are good rules. They provide useful guidelines in life. Unfortunately, though, each of these rules can encourage the development of rage patterns.

Let's start with "do what our parents do." This is called *modeling*. Children instinctively model their parents' behavior, copying their words, actions, gestures, beliefs, fears, ways of smiling and frowning—just about everything their parents do. Just last weekend, for example, David and Christopher, my two grandsons, told me all about the great fishing trip they just had gone on with their dad. They described in detail all the fish they had caught, what those fish did when hooked, and how they had measured them to decide if they were keepers. During that time, those two kids looked and sounded almost exactly like their father.

Parental modeling like that is wonderful. But what happens when parents regularly fly into rages? These parents follow the motto "when the going gets tough, have a meltdown." They throw things around. Break stuff. Scream and yell. Beat people up. Maybe they apologize later, saying how sorry they are, how they never meant to scare or hurt anybody, how they'll never do it again. Then they have another rage, and another. Their children learn that raging is how you do life.

Not everyone who grows up with raging parents, grandparents, or other significant adults becomes a rager. It is just that the odds of becoming a rager are higher if you have grown up with a raging parent.

The children may hate this rage pattern. They may even grow into adults who swear they won't become aggressive or violent like their parents. But raging parents sneak into the minds of children at unconscious levels. Later, years later, these children who are now adults may suddenly snap just like mommy or daddy did.

Marinda is one of those people. She came to counseling because one day, without warning, she had raged at her seven-year-old son, Timmy. Timmy had eaten a piece of pie without permission. He couldn't wait for supper. Marinda started to scold Timmy. Suddenly she began shaking, screaming, swearing, shaming. Marinda could feel that she was losing control. Fortunately, she was able to force herself out of the room. She made herself stay away from Timmy until she could calm down. "I became my mother, just like that," Marinda said, snapping her fingers. Marinda had grown up with a scary, raging mom. The last thing she wanted to be was a scary, raging mom herself. Yet, just for a minute, that's what happened. Having watched Mom all those years, Marinda had unconsciously absorbed a lesson on how to rage.

So what kind of family did you grow up in? Were any adults really angry? Did someone rage? What did you learn about anger when you were growing up?

Now let's discuss the second basic rule: people do what gets rewarded. This rule applies for raging. Here is an example. Maxie, a seventeen-year-old high school junior, has been diagnosed with various psychiatric problems, including attention-deficit/hyperactivity disorder, bipolar disorder, obsessive-compulsive disorder, and Asperger's syndrome. Like many troubled kids, his diagnosis keeps changing with every new psychologist or psychiatrist his mother brings him to see. Maxie has problems paying attention at school. He has few friends because of his erratic behavior. He also has a big rage problem. Maxie can go into a rage in a second. All you have to do is say no to him, and off he goes. It certainly seems that he cannot control this behavior, even when he is on strong doses of medicine.

But wait one minute. Why is it, then, that Maxie almost never rages in certain situations? For instance, Maxie rages in Mr. Johnson's social studies class almost once a week but has only raged once in the whole year he has attended Mr. Thorson's science class. The answer is that Mr. Johnson unintentionally rewards Maxie for his rages while Mr. Thorson does not. How? When Maxie begins having a meltdown, Mr. Johnson gets angry himself, lectures Maxie in front of the class, and then kicks him out of the room. Maxie earns the approval of his classmates because he took on the teacher. He gets lots of attention (even negative attention is better than no attention). And then he gets to fool around outside of the classroom. On the other hand, Mr. Thorson checks up on Maxie regularly. If he sees or senses that Maxie is close to raging, Mr. Thorson talks quietly with him. He's arranged a signal, so Maxie can let him know if he needs help calming down. But if Maxie does start losing control, Mr. Thorson immediately sends him out of the room. He avoids arguing with him. Then he retrieves Maxie after a few minutes and brings him back to the classroom.

No discussion of rages would be complete without talking about the payoffs for this behavior. *Payoffs* are the rewards, intended or unintended, for raging behavior. Rewards may be intended, immediate, and direct ("I start to rage and they give me what I want") or indirect and unintended (like extra attention). In either case, ragers learn that by raging, they can get what they want. I'm not saying, though, that people consciously decide to become ragers so that they can get what they want. It's just that people tend to keep doing what works. Raging becomes automatic. After a while, they get better and better at it, too, which means that the more people get rewarded for raging, the more frequently they will lose control.

One moral of this story is obvious: don't model raging for your children and don't reward anybody at any age for raging.

Here's another moral: be really honest with yourself about why you rage. Ask yourself what kinds of payoffs you get from raging. Then ask yourself if you are willing to give them up.

Raging Can Get You High

"I go looking for a fight. I seek out my rages. I like fighting, and I don't like fighting." These are the words of Demetrius, a twenty-five-year-old member of an anger management group. Demetrius has a long history of getting into trouble because of his anger. He's been arrested several times already and is facing hard prison time if he doesn't get a handle on his temper. The trouble is that Demetrius can't talk about his past anger episodes without smiling. His eyes begin shining, too. Just thinking about raging seems to make him come alive.

I've written before (in *Letting Go of Anger*) about something called *excitatory* or *addictive* anger. The fact is that anger can really turn some people on. And rage, the most intense form of anger, can get you higher than any other kind of anger. Just ask Demetrius. "Hey, guys, I gotta tell you. Rage is as good as sex. Maybe better."

Demetrius craves his rage. He can only go so long without raging before he goes looking for a fight. Anybody will do: his 95-pound girlfriend, his best buddy, or the 350-pound former pro football player sitting at the bar. They're all the same to him. First he gets himself angry. Then he gets in their face, hoping they'll throw the first punch. Either way, he'll attack. Taste the blood. Feel the pain. Lose his mind. Yes!

I call this anger "excitatory" because it triggers an adrenaline rush. But I also call it "addictive," because it's awfully hard to give up once you've trained yourself to feel good this way.

Now Demetrius can challenge this addictive pattern. He can learn to live without raging, just as others must figure out how to get along without alcohol, or speed, or gambling. His goal would be never to rage. As desperately as he wants excitement, as badly as he craves that intensity, as hungry as he is for rage, he must find another path in life. He could find other, more positive ways to handle his excitement (such as a job as an emergency medical technician or any other career with frequent strongly emotional or physical crises). Or Demetrius could redirect his energy toward finding ways to enjoy calm activities. He might try relaxation or meditation, for example. That kind of feeling, serenity, won't come easily to someone like Demetrius, of course. Still, he could discover that life is good even when you aren't high.

Do you get high by raging? If so, is it worth it?

Too Much Shame

Shame: a sense that something is wrong with you at the very core of your being. My wife Pat and I wrote a book on shame several years ago called *Letting Go of Shame*. It began with a story of a little girl who is having a great time making mud pies. Imagine a kid about two years old, sitting in her good dress in the backyard after a rainy day, creating wonderful buildings out of mud. But then her mother spots her. She comes running out of the house: "Shame on you. You're dirty. You're a bad girl. Shame on you."

Now imagine scenes like that being repeated throughout that girl's childhood. Before she escapes her home, that girl will have heard "shame on you" hundreds of times. And there will be many shaming events, even when those words aren't spoken aloud, things like constant criticism and scowls of disgust. That little girl might easily become a grown woman who truly believes she is no good and will never be good enough.

Shame is part of just about everybody's life. Actually, a little shame is nothing terrible. In fact, feeling shame in moderate amounts at appropriate moments is perfectly healthy. For example, I remember one time when I felt shame because, unprepared, I tried to give a talk in front of an audience. I floundered. I blushed. I wanted to run away. I felt totally exposed as a fraud. But afterwards, I made a vow always to be prepared before I give a talk. I did not want to feel that kind of shame again.

Too much shame can be quite damaging, though. Shame can become molded onto our souls. We become what the author Gershen Kaufman (1996) calls "shame bound," unable to feel good about ourselves. That feeling of intrinsic badness is terribly painful. And, what is most relevant here, excessive shame can lay the groundwork for a very dangerous kind of anger called *shame-based rage*. Shame-based rages happen when people cannot endure feeling their shame any longer. Instead, they go on the attack. They shame and blame their partners, children, friends, strangers—anyone and everyone. Their goal is to transfer their shame to others. Shame-based rage becomes a terrible game of "I don't want it, you can have it," played for the stakes of feeling good about yourself.

Shame also isolates people. Who wants to mingle with others when they feel worthless and unlikable? So, many shame-based individuals shy away from contact. They end up feeling different, unwanted, perhaps even despised. They become *marginalized*, meaning that they hang around on the fringes of groups and never feel like they belong. And, at least occasionally, these deeply shamed persons begin to despise and hate all those other people who do seem to fit in. They develop seething anger against all the goody-goodies in the world who keep them out of the mainstream. And sometimes, in a sudden blast of fury, they attack specific individuals whom they see as their main tormentors. They may also go after entire groups and institutions that, they think, keep them in the position of being have-nots in a world full of haves. That's when they go on a *rampage*, a physical attack against a group, organization, or institution.

Too Many Losses

There is another kind of life experience that produces fertile ground for the development of rage. That is the experience of too many or too intense losses.

We all know that loss is an inevitable part of life. Loved ones die. Friends move away. Couples sometimes get divorced. Children grow up and leave home. We grieve and move on. But there is one kind of loss that never feels right and is especially hard to move on from. That loss is called *abandonment*. Abandonments feel like unnecessary losses, like arbitrary decisions made by somebody just to hurt us by going away. The sense of abandonment carries with it a searing question: "Why did you leave me?" All too often, there is no reason anyone could give that would comfort the abandoned person. How do you explain to a six-year-old boy why his daddy won't be coming home from Iraq? What can you say to a forty-year-old wife whose husband has just left her for a younger woman? People sometimes become haunted by these unanswerable questions. They can't let go of them. They can't get on with their lives. They feel an emptiness they cannot endure. And that psychological vacuum opens space for rages to grow.

This kind of rage develops when people quit asking and start blaming. That's when "why did you leave me?" becomes "you should be punished for leaving me." The result is an *abandonment rage*, a furious assault against specific people who have gone away, or perhaps against anyone who reminds the abandoned person of his or her losses, or perhaps against an entire world full of people who "say they love me but always go away." Abandonment ragers are a blend of distrust, hate, and yearning. They distrust everyone who might abandon and betray them. They hate people for leaving them. And they yearn to be loved, cared for, and kept safe from harm.

Shame-based rage, rampage, and abandonment rage are important topics. Each will be discussed in greater detail later in this book.

A Vulnerability to Rage

Here is a checklist of what makes people more likely to rage. Check off the items on the list that apply to you.

- [ ] I am under twenty-five years old.

- [ ] As a child, I exploded, raged, lost control, or became violent more often (or much worse) than other children.

- [ ] I may have some brain injury (from falls, fights, accidents, etc.).

- [ ] My brain seems to shut down or work poorly when I become angry or upset.

☐ I tend to get really angry and upset when I'm under a lot of stress.

☐ I have a history of physical or emotional trauma that has left me feeling scared, vulnerable, or defensive.

☐ I have problems controlling my anger when I drink alcohol or take other mood-altering substances.

☐ I have had or am currently taking prescribed medications that seem to make me more prone to rages.

☐ I saw and heard my parents (or other important adults) raging when I was young.

☐ I got what I wanted as a child by becoming furious and losing control.

☐ I still get what I want by raging or threatening to lose control.

☐ I get high off my rages. They help me feel alive, alert, or good.

☐ I react very strongly to situations in which I feel shamed (put down, embarrassed, humiliated).

☐ I react very strongly to situations in which I feel abandoned, rejected, or betrayed.

Sudden Rage

Ricky the Sudden Rager

Here's the story of one man's strong sudden rage. His name is Ricky. He's twenty-four years old, Hispanic, a proud man with a quick temper: "I wasn't working. I couldn't find work nowhere. I was barely getting by. It was early in the day. My ex-girlfriend came by. We had an argument. She got in my face, and then she put her hands on me. She put her hands on me! That's when I exploded. I can't even remember what we were fighting about. I wasn't myself. I became a monster! I grabbed her and choked her. We were going back and forth with blows. I choked her until she blacked out. I don't remember what I said. I was thinking I was teaching her a lesson, not to get in my way. I felt very upset, just furious. I didn't even try to stop. I did stop, though, and walked around my neighborhood for a few hours. I was exhausted and went to sleep. This happens to me a lot when I'm in situations I can't control."

Sudden Rage and Loss of Control

Sudden rage is a rapidly appearing, unplanned, and unanticipated transformative anger experience during which a person may lose partial or complete control over his or her thoughts, feelings, and actions.

The content of Ricky's rages centers around the theme of loss of control. His ex-girlfriend threatened Ricky's sense of control by "getting into my face and touching me." This is a form of impotent rage (covered in chapter 6). This chapter will focus upon how Ricky rages, not why. Ricky's rages perfectly fit into the pattern of sudden rage. His anger comes on both quickly and intensely. He doesn't plan to have a rage. Instead, it feels to Ricky as if raging happens to him without warning. True, there were signs in this case that he could blow, in particular his statement that he was out of a job and pretty desperate. But Ricky said he had been okay that day until the argument with his ex-girlfriend. There was no warning he was about to have a meltdown.

When Ricky rages, he loses control over what he says and does. Notice, however, that even in the midst of this rage episode, Ricky didn't lose total control ("I didn't even try to stop. I did stop, though"). As serious as this sudden rage was, it still was only a partial rage. If he'd had a total rage, Ricky's ex-girlfriend might be dead. When Ricky rages, he becomes instantly furious, so angry that he cannot keep his rage from taking over control of his mind and body. Sometimes he blacks out, unable later to remember much or all of what he has done. Ricky mentioned when we talked that his friends joke about his anger. They all say he acts crazy and strange when he gets mad. "It's your eyes," they say. Ricky's eyes get weird when he rages, looking both glazed over and brilliant. Ricky admits that he feels like a different person when he rages, as if he were somebody else.

All this bothers Ricky a lot. But what really concerns him is the danger that he could seriously harm or kill someone during a rage. "I really hurt my ex that day. I didn't let go of her until she blacked out. And now I don't even remember what we were arguing about."

Mini Sudden Rages

Let's compare rages to black holes for a moment. Astronomers have discovered many black holes in the universe, places where gravity is so strong not even light can get out. That's why they're called black holes, of course. Many of these incredible sites are monstrously large. Some of them could contain millions of stars the size of our sun. Needless to say, these structures have received a lot of attention over the last couple of decades just because they are so gigantic. Lately, though, physicists have been pondering the idea that there may be billions of tiny, tiny black holes that pop in and out of existence. They last only briefly (fractions of a second), and they don't do much. But there they are. In fact, there may be far more of these mini black holes than big ones.

Sudden rages are like black holes because it is possible that people have far more mini-rages than monster blowouts. It's important to realize that not all sudden rages are violent like Ricky's. Nor do they all last for hours. Perhaps the best example of this occurs when someone says this: "Gee, I don't know what happened. We were arguing about money, and I just snapped! I swore at her and then I stomped off to my room. The whole thing only lasted a minute, and then I felt like an absolute idiot." That "I snapped" is a sign that this person had a mini-rage. It felt to him, just for a moment, that he wasn't exactly himself. Not that he completely lost conscious awareness, nor did he lose his sense of his normal self. Yes, he was himself, but at the same time, he could sense right then that he was also not quite himself. He had an incomplete transformation.

This is a little tricky. You could have a rage experience that is less powerful than some normal anger episodes. The issue isn't just the strength of the event but its deeper nature. When someone feels, if only for the briefest of moments, that he or she has become a different person while angry, that person is going through rage.

Strong sudden rages drive many people like Ricky to get help. That's good, because this kind of raging is dangerous. But what if you have frequent though smaller mini-rages? My suggestion is that you also would benefit greatly by learning everything you can about preventing them. Even small rages damage your relationships with others and your self-esteem. They may also eventually lead to progressively more intense and longer-lasting rage episodes as your brain learns to lose control.

Are You a Sudden Rager?

How much do you see yourself in Ricky? How often do you have smaller mini-rages? Ask yourself these questions:

- "Does my anger come on both very quickly and very intensely?"

- "Do I get so angry that I lose control over what I say or do?"

- "Do people say I act strange, scary, or crazy when I get really mad?"

- "Have I blacked out (not from alcohol or drugs) when I became very angry, so I did not remember things I said or did?"

- "Do I get so angry that I worry I might seriously harm or kill someone?"

- "Do I feel like I become a different person when I get angry—as if I am not really myself?"

- "Do I become instantly furious when I feel that somebody has insulted or threatened me?"

- "Do I snap, even for a short period, when I get angry?"

If you do see yourself as a sudden rager, then you will probably want to pay close attention to the rest of this chapter. The topic is how to prevent sudden raging.

How to Stop Sudden Raging

Here are seven steps you can take to stop sudden raging.

STEP 1. *Be hopeful. Believe that you can learn how to stop raging.*

It's easy to feel pretty hopeless when it comes to stopping raging. Why? Because a lot of times, rages, especially sudden rages, just seem to happen. It's like you're at a restaurant and the waiter suddenly shows up with a five-pound steak. "Who ordered this?" you ask, and the waiter says, "You did, and here's the bill." That humongous steak is your rage, and the bill is what it's going to cost you after you're done with it.

The idea here is to tell the waiter, "Wait a minute. I didn't order that steak. I don't want it. And I won't accept it at my table. Take it back to the kitchen." Maybe the waiter will argue with you, insisting that the steak is yours. Perhaps, he'll say that the last time you were here, you ordered one just that size. He might even tell you they've been saving their biggest steak just for you because they know how much you appreciate it. But don't let that waiter argue you into taking it. You don't need that kind of meal anymore.

There is one very important difference between the waiter who brings you a steak and the waiter who brings you a rage. The first waiter lives in his own house. The second waiter resides in your head. And that's where all your rages begin. Inside your head. Inside your brain. But that's good. It's your head, your brain. They belong to you. And you can change what goes on inside that brain of yours. Maybe not all the time. Maybe not perfectly. But enough to make your life a whole lot better.

Whatever you do, do not give up on yourself. You can stop raging.

STEP 2. *Make a commitment to work hard and long to contain your rage.*

Get ready for some hard work. Stopping yourself from raging is no easy job. First, you'll have to let go of your defenses and be totally honest with yourself. This means:

- No more denial. Not, "Aw, I don't know what they're talking about. I don't have a rage problem." Instead, "Yes, I have a big problem in my life. It's called rage. I admit it. I accept it. And I've got to do something, right now, about it."

- No more minimization. Not, "Well, maybe I do have a little anger problem, but it's nothing I can't control." Instead, "Little problem, my ass! This is huge. My rages are destroying my life. I'm hurting my kids. My raging is ruining everything."

- No more rationalizations or justifications. Not, "Yeah, I rage, but it's not my fault. It's all because my dad beat me when I was a kid." Instead, "Sure, Dad beat me. But that was years ago. I have to take responsibility for myself now. I won't blame my present on the past anymore."

- No more pleas of helplessness or hopelessness. Not, "I just can't stop, so why even bother to try?" Instead, "I'm not sure how much control I can get over these rages, but I'm going to work at it. My goal is stopping every one of them."

- No more stalling. Not, "I know I should work on these rages. But I'm not ready. Maybe next year." Instead, "Now's the time to start working on stopping these rages. I can't afford to screw up any longer."

Secondly, you'll need to learn everything you can about when, how, why, where, and with whom you rage. You'll need to become a scientist doing research on your rage patterns. And next, after you learn as much as you can about your own unique rage patterns, you'll need to design and practice a personalized set of rage-stopping skills.

What comes after that? Putting your knowledge to use. That means actually stopping your rages from even beginning, whenever you can (prevention), or at least slowing them down and making them less damaging, if you can't stop them (containment).

Don't expect perfection. You can't stop raging just by snapping your fingers or waving a magic wand. But do expect to make fairly rapid progress. It's reasonable for you to believe that you can get better and better at containing your rages, beginning right now, as you read this book. You will need to make a very strong commitment, though, to keep working on this problem consistently, day after day, week after week.

STEP 3. *Take the time to identify your sudden-rage patterns.*

The goal is for you to learn as much as you can about the unique way you rage. The following set of questions will help you recognize your sudden-rage patterns. Please take the time to really think about these questions. Write down your answers on a separate sheet of paper.

Here is a place for you to describe a particular sudden rage you have gone through. This exercise is designed to help you gather information on how you rage so that you can better quit raging.

1. About how long ago did this event take place?

2. What was going on in your life at the time that added stress to your life or might help explain what happened?

3. Had you been drinking or drugging right before or during the rage (or withdrawing from a heavy period of intoxication)? If so, how do you think that affected you?

4. Who was involved in the rage episode?

5. What triggered the rage (maybe something someone said or did)?

6. How much of what happened during the rage did you remember the next day (all, some, none at all)? If you remember anything, what do you remember?

7. During the rage, what did you say? What did you think? What did you feel? What did you do?

8. How did the rage end?

9. How hard did you try to stay in control before or during the rage? What did you do to keep control? Did it work?

10. Would you say that, during the rage, you were completely out of control, partly out of control, mostly in control, completely in control? Would you call what you went through a near rage, partial rage, or total rage? Why?

11. What happened to you after the sudden rage (for example, did you sleep for hours, get arrested, or did your wife leave you)? Describe whatever happened.

12. How often do you experience sudden rages?

13. Are you taking any medications to help control your anger, emotions, or rages? If so, what are they? Do they help?

14. What else do you do to prevent or control your rages?

15. What else could you write that would help you describe and understand your rages?

STEP 4. *Look at your past near-rage episodes to learn more about how you sometimes prevent yourself from sudden raging.*

Tonya, a twenty-year-old group-home resident, recently told me about a near-rage episode. Tonya had been arguing with Mike, another resident, about chores. Tonya insisted that it was Mike's turn to do the dishes. Mike refused to do them. Tonya could feel her anger building, and building, and building. She could feel the adrenaline starting to pump. She *wanted* to explode. Tonya felt like sticking a knife into Mike's chest and laughing all the way to jail. But then, just like that, she completely stopped the rage. She walked away. She went to her room to cool down.

At first, Tonya said that she didn't know how she did it. But then, after she thought a while, here's what she said: "I told myself it wasn't worth it. Mike's an ass. He'll always be an ass. So why try to change him? He's not gonna change. Besides, I'm not Mike's boss. Let the staff deal with him. They get paid to handle asses." Of course, the staff had probably said exactly those words to Tonya a hundred times. But she didn't hear them. She didn't want to hear them. Tonya wanted to be in control. But now, she was hearing herself speak, not the staff. And she liked what she was saying to herself. So she listened. That's how she stopped a rage from happening.

A *near rage* is an event during which a person gets very close to an uncontrollable sudden rage but then is able to stop. Probably everyone who rages has several near-rage episodes for every time he or she lets loose with a total uncontrolled rage. If not, that person is almost certainly locked up safely behind bars and/or tranquilized to near-vegetable status with heavy-duty medications. Raging is simply too dangerous for society to tolerate.

This means that even if you are a rager, you know how to decline a rage. So what's your secret? How do you keep yourself from raging most of the time?

What do you think that keeps you from raging? Like Tonya, do you say to yourself, "It isn't worth it"? Do you tell yourself to calm down? If not, what do you say to yourself that helps?

What do you do physically when rages threaten? Do you walk away? Sit down? Take a few deep breaths? What else do you do?

What do you do with your anger when you keep yourself from raging? Do you stuff it? Ignore it? Try to be assertive but not aggressive? Try just to let it go? Notice your other emotions? What else do you do with your anger?

Do you have any spiritual strategies to help you not rage? Pray? Let go and let God? Meditate? Go to church? What else?

Do you get immediate help from family, friends, professionals, or fellow travelers? Perhaps you call up a friend ("Joe, do you have a minute? I've got to talk to you right now"). Maybe you have a counselor you particularly trust whom you can see on short notice when you're close to raging. Perhaps you belong to a self-help group such as Emotions Anonymous or Alcoholics Anonymous, where you can meet and speak with others also trying to contain their rages.

Learn everything you can about how you stop your sudden rages before they even begin. After all, you are the expert on you. Who knows you better?

STEP 5. *Look at your partial-rage episodes
to learn more about how you stay at least
somewhat in control even during a sudden rage.*

Lucy is the mother of Jerry and Jed, twelve-year-old twins. The other day, the cops came looking for the twins, accusing them of selling marijuana to their middle school classmates. Now Lucy knows that Jerry and Jed smoke weed. She's not happy about it, but she hasn't been able to stop them. However, she had no idea they were dealing.

Things were going okay until a young social worker named Michelle showed up. Michelle fully intended to pull Jed and Jerry from the home. She told them to get in her car, so she could bring them to a shelter. That's when Lucy blew. She swore at Michelle. She screamed at her kids to run and hide. She threatened Michelle and the police. She began melting down as she had often done in the past.

But then, somehow, some way, Lucy regained control. She kept swearing but stopped screaming. She kept arguing loudly but quit telling the kids to run. Basically, Lucy chose to keep her gloves on instead of fighting bare-knuckled. The result was that Lucy only had a partial rage.

How did she do that? Lucy says that she realized she had to stop for the sake of the twins. "I was making things worse for them. I could see that. Besides, I knew I couldn't help them if I was in jail or in a mental unit. So I made myself stop. Believe me, it wasn't easy. But I did it."

A *partial rage* is an event in which a person begins to rage but still maintains some control over what is occurring. The key question to ask yourself, if you've ever had a partial rage, is this: "What did I think to myself, say, or do that kept me at least partly in control?" That's a very important question. Knowing the answer could literally keep you from severely hurting or killing someone in the future.

So once again, consider these questions. During your partial rages, what do you think that keeps you from totally losing control when you begin raging? What do you do physically to contain a rage? What do you do with your anger? Do you have any spiritual strategies to help you keep some control over your rages? Do you get immediate help from family, friends, professionals, or fellow travelers? Is there anything anyone can do to help you during a partial rage? Is it better if people just leave you alone?

STEP 6. *Make a safety plan to lessen your risk for sudden raging. A safety management plan might include gathering a support system, getting anger management training, and possibly taking appropriate medication.*

Get a support system. "Come on, Benny, let's get out of here." *The scene*: three guys sitting on bar stools at a tavern around midnight. Two of the men are exchanging angry words. *The players*: Benny, an easily irritated guy who becomes a rager when drunk, his best friend Darren, who has seen Benny go crazy many times before, and an obviously intoxicated man who doesn't know either of them but is ready for a brawl. *The music:* drumrolls in the background becoming louder and louder as the tension builds. *The result:* Darren convinces Benny to leave the tavern before Benny starts raging, while he can still stay in control.

Now this result is certainly anticlimactic. It won't get Benny and Darren on *Oprah* or Dr. Phil's show. But what it does is keep one foolish drunk out of the hospital or morgue and Benny out of jail.

Friends. Family. Spouse or partner. Priests, ministers, rabbis. Fellow self-help group members. Counselors. Doctors. These people are absolutely necessary if you want to quit raging. Don't try to go it alone, because it won't work. Why? Because when people get close to a rage, they tend to speak nonsense to themselves: "Watch out! They're out to get me! I wanna kill that S.O.B.! He deserves it! Nobody says that to me! I can't live without her! He's putting me down! I hate them! I'm not drunk! It's payback time!" These are not the thoughts of a reasonable person. They are the words of people working themselves into a rage.

People heading into a rage need others who can calm them, get them away from danger, and help talk them down. So gather a support system and, most importantly, use it.

Get anger management training. You may ask, "What's the use of teaching me anger management skills? What good will it do if I get so mad I can't think? Isn't medication the only thing that can help?" The answer, I believe, is that you should learn as many anger management skills as you can. Anger management training provides motivation as well as specific skills. It helps you become motivated to control your rages and provides ways to do exactly that. Anger management can help you change negative habits of thinking and feeling that lay the groundwork for rage. Once you have anger management training, you may be able to cut off completely at least some of your rages while lessening the intensity of others. As for skill training versus medication, it may not be an either/or question. You may need to both learn anger management skills and take medication.

There are four main ways you may need to change, so you can gain better control over your anger.

1. Change what you do.

2. Change what you think.

3. Change how you react to stress.

4. Change your spirit.

First, change what you do. For Benny, that means staying away from bars, because that's where all his rages occur. Avoiding trouble spots is one change many ragers need to make. Taking a time-out is another important way to change your behavior. A good time-out features the four Rs: *recognize* that you are getting dangerously mad, *retreat* before you say or do something stupid, *relax* until the anger drains away, and then *return* to deal in a reasonable manner with the situation that upset you (Potter-Efron 2001).

Fair fighting is another classic anger management tool. Here you make a commitment to handle conflicts without swearing, name-calling, bullying, threatening, and so on. You sit down, stay calm, really listen to the other person, and seek positive solutions, instead of just demanding other people do things your way.

Change what you think. Wally, a forty-five-year-old physician, is a road rager. Once Wally got so mad at another driver, he followed him for five miles, honking his horn and shaking his fist the whole time. What had the other driver done? He had passed Wally just as they were entering a no-passing zone. Wally became furious. What he thought was this: "He can't do that! It's against the law. I won't let him get away with that." And off he charged, becoming, as he said, a "traffic vigilante."

Now most of what is called "road rage" is really just road anger. People get mad and give each other the finger, then go their own ways. But Wally really was raging. He was so mad, he couldn't think. He was more than ready for a fight. He was willing to turn the highway into a demolition derby. Fortunately, the other driver did not react to aggression with aggression. Eventually, Wally came to his senses and drove away.

Wally worked on what is labeled *disputation* to help him quit road raging. A simpler name is the A-B-C-D-E technique (Potter-Efron 2001). It looks like this:

A = The antecedent. That's whatever is happening that you get angry about.

B = The negative beliefs you have that increase your anger about this situation.

C = The consequences of your anger. What you do because you're angry.

D = The disputation. A new, anger-reducing thought that you substitute for B.

E = The effects of your new thought. That usually means letting go of your anger or figuring out something useful to do with it.

Here's what Wally did to dispute his old way of thinking:

A: The driver passed him just as they reached a no-passing zone. I call that an *anger invitation*. Wally usually accepts these anger invitations all too eagerly.

B: Wally's main anger-increasing belief in this situation was that anyone who drives badly is an idiot who should be punished. Furthermore, Wally felt he had the right to be the punisher (the "road vigilante").

C: That's when Wally began chasing after the other guy.

D: Disputations are the most important part of this process. You must come up with a new thought you can substitute for the old one. Furthermore, that new thought must feel right to you. It has to help you calm down. Here was Wally's new thought: "Hey, I'm not the world's designated traffic cop. I'm a doctor, not a vigilante. I don't need to take this on."

E: Now when something like this happens, Wally repeats these new thoughts to himself and relaxes. He's more comfortable with himself, and he actually feels better on the road. Most importantly, he might be saving someone's life, including his own, by keeping himself from raging.

Change how you react to stress.   Wally, like many anger-prone people, has a strong bodily reaction to even slightly stressful situations. When that driver cut in on him, he instantly had a fight-or-flight response. Adrenaline was released; Wally's heart started pounding; his breathing quickened; his thinking capacity dropped as his brain shifted into emergency gear. Wally could have cut that reaction off, though. He needed to realize what was going on, take a few slow, deep breaths, tell himself it was no big deal, and relax. Of course, it's a lot easier to say that than for Wally to actually do it at the moment of truth. But if Wally worked at it, he certainly could train himself to help his body relax instead of go into action-alert status.

Relaxation training is the key to changing your reaction to stress. This type of training takes many forms: classic deep-muscle relaxation, meditation, yoga, breathing exercises, and so on. It takes practice and repetition to get it right, though. You can't just take a few deep breaths every once in a while.

I believe that relaxation training is valuable both for rage prevention and containment. Prevention means that you don't get angry in the first place. Regularly practicing relaxation helps you start the day in a better mood. It helps you feel more in control of your own body. So when something annoying does happen, you know what to do. You can turn down anger invitations just by taking a couple of deep breaths.

Relaxation also helps contain anger. You contain anger when you get angry but don't go crazy. Okay, you accept the anger invitation. But you don't have a meltdown. You don't fly into a rage. You just get angry for a while, and then you let it go.

Changing how you react to stress is both physical and mental. Relaxation allows you to think. Thinking helps you solve problems. Solving problems helps you let go of your anger.

Change your spirit. Anger management is more than teaching people a specific set of skills. It also involves helping people take a good, long look at their lives. Are you happy? Content? At peace with yourself? Comfortable with your place in the world? Or are you unhappy, depressed, gloomy, hostile, anxious, and dispirited? Ragers, as you would probably guess, tend toward the latter. They often are miserably unhappy people. They may have lost hope in everyone and everything.

You, the reader, may be a rager. If so, please take the time to take an in-depth look at your life. But don't do this if you plan to use it only to blame everybody else for your troubles. That's not the point. Instead, look at what you do to make your life good or bad, happy or unhappy, positive or negative.

- Do you first look for the good in people instead of the bad?

- Do you take responsibility for your life instead of expecting others to take care of you?

- Do you show caring and give praise to others instead of being insensitive and critical?

- Do you feel like you have a purpose in life, or do you feel you're just drifting?

- Do you feel connected to your family, friends, and the community, or do you feel isolated and alienated?

- Do you have a meaningful spiritual life, in which you feel connected with a force larger than yourself?

Actions, thoughts, feelings, and spirit. These are the areas you need to change if you truly want to quit raging.

Get proper medication management. Many ragers are reluctant to take medication. They have lots of reasons for their reluctance. First, they want to be in control of their lives without having to take pills. Perhaps they are afraid of possible side effects. Maybe they just don't think their rage is really that big a problem. Another possibility is that they would have to give up alcohol or drugs to stop raging, and they don't want to quit. Maybe the payoffs they get from raging are such that they don't really want to stop. Or perhaps taking medications violates their religious principles. But the most common reason of all is that they don't think they really need medications.

Here are the counterarguments. You could kill someone if you don't quit raging. You could kill yourself. You are making life miserable for everybody. You are a loose cannon that could go off at any time. You are hurting your children by not doing everything you can to gain control over these rages. Ultimately, if you don't take medications, you may lose your partner, your family, your job, your health, your life.

Chapter 2 discussed how the brains of ragers may be less than perfect. Please reread that section carefully if you are reluctant to take medications. More directly, how can you expect to control your rages if your brain doesn't always work quite right?

Medications. Anger management. A good support system. These are the ingredients for an effective rage-breaking program.

STEP 7. *Work on your long-term issues to make permanent changes in your sense of self and the world. The goal here is to feel secure with others, good about yourself, sane, and healthy.*

People who rage often live with tremendous insecurity. The world is a scary, dangerous place. People are threatening. Relationships are fragile. Nobody can be trusted. But it's not just the world outside of yourself. Your inner universe is also shaky and uncertain: "I feel so empty. Weak. Unconfident. Incompetent. Screwed up. Helpless. Worthless." Many, if not all, ragers are insecure at the deepest level of existence.

This too must change. People who rage need to work on their personal demons. These may have involved abandonment, physical or sexual abuse, excessive criticism and shaming, traumatic incidents, or times of great powerlessness. Working on these issues might mean talking things through with good and trusted friends. It could involve going into therapy. Some people just need to read and think, to spend time alone sorting through the stories in their heads. Religious or other spiritual explorations often help. Above all, ragers need to take the time to become friends with themselves. That is the only way that their worlds can ever become safer.

Of course, a personal sense of security is not just a state of mind. People need to live in a realistically safe world in order to feel secure. You could hardly expect the Hurricane Katrina survivors who were stuck in the New Orleans Superdome to feel secure when they were thirsty, hungry, and listening to gunshots. The goal is to have external safety and internal security in your life.

If you are a sudden rager, you need to consider your long-range game plan. What exactly do you want to do with your life? How can you feel better about yourself? How can you make your world safer and more secure, both externally and internally? Set some positive goals. Plan out how to reach them. Make your life better, if only so you will be less tempted to rage.

Seething Rage, Personal Vendettas, and Rampage

Samuel's Seething Rage

Samuel is a twenty-year-old bricklayer whose seething rage began three years ago while he was doing time for a series of armed robberies. Here's his story:

> "I was locked up, and I started withdrawing from a very heavy period of total intoxication. It affected me because I was extremely irritable and I had no control over the situation. That's when my significant other wrote me a letter telling me she was dating my best friend and also that she was living with him at his house. At first, I could accept it. I was going to be in prison for three years, so what right did I have to keep her? But I kept reading that letter over and over, and this rage began building inside of me. I was

on lockdown in my cell, and that just added more fuel to the fire. I was so angry, I wanted to destroy everything, and I kept thinking about the two of them together, and it was making me sick. I ended up getting into a fight with my cell mate just because he was in the cell with me and I had to take it out on someone. But that didn't help. I've hung on to that rage for so long now. Sometimes it fades away for a while, and the only reason it fades away is because of the amount of time that has passed. But then it comes back stronger than before. There are times I just space out and purposely bring the rage back to keep me mad and aggressive. I spend hours plotting revenge, thinking of ways to hurt them. I try to talk myself out of it, but it's no use. All I want to do when I get out of here is to make them suffer like they've made me suffer."

This isn't the first time Samuel has felt this kind of seething rage. In fact, he has developed a habit of raging: "I tend to hang on to past resentments as a way to have my revenge in the future. I know it's not healthy for me to hold grudges, because it is always painful for me and the other person in the end. The only advice I can offer someone with a rage problem like mine is to seek help, because the rage only gets worse."

How Seething Rage Differs from Sudden Rage

Most of the people described in this book so far would say their rages occur quickly and with little warning. They experience sudden rage. But there is another kind of experience people also call rage. This second type of rage develops differently. The main rage-producing problems—survival, impotence, shame, and abandonment—are still there, but the threats are usually both slower building and longer lasting. The name for this second type of experience is seething rage.

Sudden rages are usually a reaction to an immediate frustration. Not so with seething rages, which are more reactions against past insults and injuries. Seething rages build more slowly in response to what someone feels is a terribly unfair situation. These rages are like underground fires, smoldering below your full consciousness for years before they finally break through to the surface.

Rages, then, basically occur in two main forms. On the one hand, a rage may develop suddenly and furiously, like a tornado appearing from nowhere, destructively twisting itself through people's lives, and then disappearing as quickly as it came. That is a sudden rage. Certainly, sudden rages are both common and alarming. They demand attention because of their immediate visibility and power. Nobody can ignore someone going through a sudden rage. But there is another important way that people rage. Here, the storm develops slowly, usually with plenty of warning, but it still cannot be stopped. If sudden rages are like unscheduled tornadoes, then these seething rages are more like the highly predictable monsoons that strike Asia every year.

What Is Seething Rage?

A seething rage is a long-term buildup of fury toward a specific individual or cluster of individuals. The components of seething rage include a sense of having been victimized, obsessive thoughts about the situation, moral outrage and hatred toward the offenders, vengeful fantasies, and (sometimes) deliberately planned assaults upon targeted offenders.

Samuel is experiencing a seething rage. He is unable to quit thinking about his injury. It just keeps coming up in his brain, even when he tries to think of something else. Furthermore, his anger keeps growing over time. He harbors fantasies of revenge against those people who have harmed him, in this case his ex–significant other and his ex–best friend. As his anger builds, it turns into out-and-out hatred. There is also a belief about having been betrayed by those he had trusted and even a sense of moral indignation or outrage. Moral indignation is a particularly dangerous component of a seething rage. It makes Samuel into an innocent victim and his ex into a monster, devil, or simply evil person who should be destroyed. Samuel, like most people with seething rages, has trouble forgiving those who have offended him. People with this kind of rage almost always have to deal with a tremendously strong sense that the offender or offenders who have harmed them are morally bad, monstrous, and evil.

By the way, do you think Samuel will tell the parole board about his thoughts of revenge? Of course not, because he knows he'd get in big trouble and maybe be kept in prison indefinitely. It is typical of people with seething rages to hide from others the full strength of their outrage. This makes the rage difficult to spot, because so much of the rager's fury lies hidden from view. However, detection is important, for the stakes are high here. All too often, the rager's defenses finally break down, releasing years of pent-up fury. That's when this person may become extremely dangerous, especially if he or she has developed plans on how to exact revenge.

Personal Vendettas and Rampages

Samuel's rage is directed against two people, his former significant other and his former best friend. He believes they betrayed him. He can't quit thinking about them. He desires vengeance. These people have become his mortal enemies. He cannot rest until he gets back at them.

The most common seething rage is like Samuel's. It is a *personal vendetta* in which you vow eternal war against a mortal enemy who is held responsible for your suffering. Perhaps the best example in literature of a personal vendetta is Captain Ahab, who, in Herman Melville's famous novel, *Moby-Dick*, dies trying to kill his personal nemesis, the white whale. On a lighter note, the pirate captain in the tale of Peter Pan also has a personal nemesis—the crocodile with an alarm clock in his belly.

However, there is another kind of seething rage that has become particularly scary in the last few years. These rages occur when people attack institutions as well as individuals. Several years ago, these rages were called "going postal," after a few incidents in which postal workers besieged their workplaces. But more recently, the attackers have been teenagers, and the institution they've attacked has been their high schools.

The label for this type of rage is a *rampage*, which is a seething rage directed in fantasy or reality against a specific institution, such as a school, business, or government agency, that is held primarily responsible for the offenses against the rager.

Some of the research on rampages helps to clarify the differences between anger and rage. Katherine Newman (2004) notes that young-sters who commit acts of rampage tend not to be the obviously angry children and teenagers who get kicked out of classes a lot and get in trouble with the law. Instead, these youths more often are outsiders (or at least see themselves as outsiders)—the kids who don't quite fit in with others, the ones who exist on the fringes of school life. Newman writes that these students usually don't attract much atten-tion from teachers, counselors, or school administrators. Basically, nobody recognizes that they are slowly building resentments, not just toward one or two persons but against the whole school. They hate other students for excluding them, teachers for ignoring them, and administrators for having power over them. Eventually, their hate overwhelms them and they attack "the system," typically by showing up one day and randomly shooting at students and teachers.

Are You a Seething Rager?

Seething rages are always dangerous, whether directed at specific targets or larger groups. Ask yourself the following questions to help determine if seething rages are or could become a problem for you.

- Are you unable to quit thinking about past insults or injuries?

- Does your anger about some past insult sometimes seem to grow greater over time, instead of leveling off or diminishing?

- Do you sometimes have intense fantasies of revenge against people who have harmed you?

- Do you hate people for what they have done to you?

- Would people be amazed if they knew how angry you get, even though you don't show it?

- Do you feel outraged about what people try to get away with?

- Do you have difficulty forgiving people?

- Do you "seethe" in anger but don't say anything to others?

- Do you deliberately hurt people (physically or verbally) in order to pay them back for something they did to you?

- Do you believe that any particular person (or group, organization, or institution) is to blame for your unhappiness?

- Do people tell you it's time to move on and quit dwelling on the past?

If you see yourself as a seething rager, the rest of this chapter is designed to help you.

Preventing Seething Rages

There are six main steps you can take to prevent seething rages from taking over your life.

STEP 1. *Realize you always have a choice.*

Max, Vinny, and Charles were long-time best friends and roommates. After they graduated from college, they began a business together, the Three Brothers Organic Foods restaurant. The name of the restaurant said it all—they were as close as brothers, full of love and trust for each other. But then Charles got into gambling. At first, he just made an occasional trip to the casino with friends. Then he began going three times a week, then daily. He started chasing his losses. Charles burned through every dollar of cash and credit he had. Soon, he was playing the slots on company money. By the time Max and Vinny discovered the problem, the restaurant could not be saved. Charles was charged with embezzlement. But instead of Charles doing jail time, his attorney worked out a diversion agreement. Charles did thirty days at a treatment center and a year in a halfway house. He was able to quit gambling and rebuild his life. He joined Gambler's Anonymous, a self-help organization.

Charles has been working through the steps of his self-help recovery program. He has reached a place in his life where he wants to make amends to Max and Vinny. He even developed a plan to pay each of them several thousand dollars, restitution for some of the harm he caused. That's why he tried calling each of them to arrange a meeting. This is where choice enters the picture: Max and Vinny each had a choice about how to respond to Charles.

Here is what Max said: "Charles, yes, I'll meet with you. I've thought of you often. I still have some bad feelings about what you did, of course, but I also think about what a good person you are. Come on over." Turns out that Max has begun a new venture during this last year and a half. He's managing an organic foods cooperative, with the hope of beginning another restaurant within a couple of years. He says that he isn't about to let Charles destroy his life: "That's over and done with. If I kept on wailing about what Charles did, I would just be wallowing in misery."

Vinny had an entirely different response: "Charles, I will never forgive you for what you did. You were a traitor. You betrayed me. You ruined my life. I will always hate you. I think about what you did to me every day. You could never repay me enough, so don't bother trying. And don't come over here. If you do, I'll beat the crap out of you!"

Seething rages are festering wounds. The more you scratch at them, the more they bleed. The longer they last, the more damage they do. Eventually, an untreated seething rage scars your soul, just as an untreated wound disfigures the body.

That's Vinny. He is raging, not in the quick manner of a sudden rage, but slowly, slowly, slowly. He wakes up at night stewing over the loss of the restaurant. He is so full of hate toward Charles, he can taste it. Vinny has fantasies about beating or even killing Charles. Nor does he want to let it go, to put this terrible deed into the past. It's as if Vinny prefers being the long-suffering victim to getting on with his life. His rage is a wound that won't heal. The result? While Max has left the past behind, Vinny is stuck in it. He hasn't gotten a decent job since the restaurant's demise. He talks endlessly, to anyone who will listen, about how Charles ruined his life. Mostly, Vinny sits around feeling hopeless, angry, and depressed. And here's the scary part. Vinny has become even more irate since Charles called. "What right does Charles have to be walking around the neighborhood a free man after what he did? That's not right. That's not fair. Somebody should do something about it." Lately, Vinny has been driving by the place where he thinks Charles lives. He's considering his options, from starting to call Charles at two every morning, just to annoy him, to knifing his tires to…? Who knows what Vinny is capable of in this rageful state?

If only Vinny realized he still has a choice. He doesn't have to spend hours every day picking open his old wounds. He could quit scratching. Instead, he keeps himself stuck in a victim stance. Unlike Max, who is doing well because he has gone on with his life, Vinny is miserable because he has allowed his seething rage to control his life. You, too, have a choice if you are prone to seething rage. Will you be like Max or like Vinny?

STEP 2. *Consciously choose to move toward peace of mind, rather than discontent, to prevent rages from developing.*

Seething rages always take time to develop. Think of sand trickling through the neck of an hourglass. Now, let the top half of the hourglass represent the kind of peace of mind that people enjoy when they are free from resentments. The feelings usually associated with this state are calm, serene, happy, or content. Now let the bottom half of the glass become the exact opposite, a place of discontent, unhappiness, misery, and self-pity. The bottom half of the hourglass is where you are building a seething rage. Each particle of sand trickling down stands for a new grain of frustration, unresolved conflict, moral indignation, or perceived humiliation you are feeling. Some of these grains are about injuries you suffered long ago. Others are more immediate. The number of grains increases only gradually, maybe over weeks, months, or even years. Nevertheless, after a while there are an awful lot of them. The more that glass of discontent fills, the worse you feel. And if you let all those grains of animosity fall into the bottom half of the glass, you'll blow up and rage.

Don't just stand there watching your anger turn into a seething rage. Do something! Turn that hourglass over. Instead of representing problems, the grains of sand now stand for conflicts you've resolved, positive solutions to life's continuing issues, and feelings of contentment. With every falling grain, you're increasing your peace of mind while decreasing your potential for rage.

This hourglass analogy reminds me of something I believe deeply: life is always getting better or getting worse. Seething rage can only occur when you've let your life get worse for a long time.

Turning that hourglass over is a revolutionary process. It will help you feel better about yourself and the world than you have in a long time. The next three steps will help you change how you think and what you do, so you can find greater contentment.

STEP 3. *Examine your current thoughts and behaviors to determine if you are developing or hanging onto any long-term resentment that could produce a seething rage.*

Seething rages develop when people cannot let go of their resentments. Perhaps someone is rude to you or forgets to call. You could think something like this: "Well, that's life. It's no big deal." And that would be the end of it. Instead, you hang onto the injury and dwell upon it. "How could they do that to me? Who do they think they are?" And then you start looking for more things to resent the person for. It takes more than a few resentments to produce a rage, of course. Certainly not everyone who carries resentments becomes a seething rager. The difference is that people who rage like this allow their injuries to build and build inside their brains until they become unendurable. They think and think and think about how people have attacked or betrayed them. They dwell on life's injustices. They seethe in anger. And, if eventually they reach an "I can't take it anymore" stage, they rage.

One way, then, to prevent raging, is to stop yourself from developing resentments. You must regularly perform a special kind of mental self-examination to do so.

Begin in the present, today. Is there anything happening right now about which you could build a resentment? An argument with your partner. A conflict at work. A dispute with your parents, siblings, or children. A physical problem that won't go away. A fight with a friend. Recent political events. Financial difficulties. The state of the universe. All these and more are the kind of things that foster the growth of seething rages.

Here's an example. Morgan and Jenny, who are roommates, have a disagreement about exactly who should pay what on the cable television bill. Morgan ordered cable last month without consulting Jenny, although Morgan thought they had agreed it would be nice to have it. Morgan says Jenny should pay half. Jenny says she didn't order cable and doesn't need it (although she watches it), so she shouldn't owe anything. Here comes this month's bill in the mail. Right at that moment, Morgan needs to consider her choices. On the one hand, she can fret and stew about this issue, turning it into a major event in her mind. But then it becomes a grain of sand trickling into the hourglass of discontent, leading toward a seething rage against Jenny. That kind of thinking could make the rest of the time they are roommates a living hell. On the other hand, Morgan could let this cable bill disagreement stay a small concern, not something to lose sleep over.

The time to stop a seething rage from growing is always *now*. The earlier, the better: before the sense of your life being ruined gets locked into your brain, before your ongoing anger sucks the joy right out of your life. So, take time every day to ask yourself this question: "Have I let myself grow a small resentment today?" If so, see if you can let it go while the resentment is still tiny. It will be much easier to do so now, rather than later when it has become larger and harder.

So what do you do once you catch yourself developing resentment? Often the best thing to do is to go directly to the person you are upset with, so you can address your concerns. Try to work things out. Perhaps there has simply been a misunderstanding that can quickly be fixed. Or maybe you have real differences, but a respectful discussion will kill that resentful feeling before it can grow.

Before seeking the other person out, though, try to sort through what is making you angry or upset. It's possible that you're getting bothered without a good reason. Also, try using the disputation technique described below. It might help you look at the situation differently.

STEP 4. *Use the disputation technique to challenge any resentment that leads you toward seething rage.*

It's one thing to identify the beginning of resentments. But how, then, can you cut them off? One way is to use the A-B-C-D-E disputation technique described in chapter 3. Just to review, the goal in any situation is to substitute a positive, anger-reducing thought for a negative, anger-increasing thought. Imagine, for example, how much better Vinny would feel if he could exchange Max's thought, "I'm not going to let Charles's actions ruin my life," for his own thought that "Charles destroyed my life. I can't go on." If he could, he wouldn't be trapped in his rage, unable to get on with his life.

You can almost always find a less angry way to look at something. Seething rages occur when you make the worst possible interpretations of what others say and do. So please review the material on disputations in chapter 3 to help you think differently.

STEP 5. *Practice empathy to lessen feelings of outrage.*

A sense of moral outrage fuels most seething rages. The people who have harmed you seem to be evil, immoral, sinful, and wicked. Empathy is the antidote for moral outrage. Empathy means putting yourself in the shoes of another person, so you can better understand how that person thinks and feels. Empathy is not the same as making excuses for someone, though. People have to be held responsible for their behavior, no matter how well you understand them or how much you feel for them. But practicing empathy pulls you out of an "I'm good and you're bad" world and into a "we're all in this together" world. Vinny could be more empathic toward Charles by learning about addictions, in general, and gambling addiction, in particular. He could do that by asking himself several questions. How did Charles get caught up in gambling? Why couldn't he stop? What was Charles thinking and feeling as he plunged deeper and deeper into that hellhole? What is he like now?

There are basically two types of empathy. The first kind involves trying to really understand another person's way of thinking. I call that *cognitive empathy*. The idea is to think about something somebody did that you didn't like, something that could begin or add to a resentment. Then try to put yourself in that person's place. If you were that person, what might you have been thinking at that time? What is most important to that person? What does he or she value, want, and need in life? The second kind of empathy is *emotional*. What was that person feeling at the time the problem occurred? Was he or she scared? Angry? Embarrassed? Sad?

Here's an example of how someone used empathy to let go of a budding resentment. His name is Sandy and his stepdaughter Bets is thirteen years old. Sandy resented the fact that Bets seldom talked with him for the first few months after he married her mother, Brianna. In fact, by walking off into her bedroom when he came home from work, Bets downright avoided him. On the other hand, Bets talked openly and enthusiastically with her mother. Sandy felt angry and hurt. To make things worse, his stepdaughter's behavior painfully reminded him of times when his parents paid more attention to his brothers than him. Sandy was heading toward a seething rage. Finally, he talked with Brianna about it. She asked him to put himself in her daughter's shoes. She reminded him that the girl's birth father despised Sandy and insisted that Bets have nothing to do with him. She pointed out that Bets was caught in the middle. "How would you feel if you were Bets?" Brianna asked Sandy. Then Sandy realized that Bets might be worried about losing her father.

Furthermore, he realized that putting pressure on Bets to be nice to him would only backfire. Sandy decided then to let her have her space and to not get angry when she walked away. Instead, he patiently waited until, a few months later, she gradually began sticking around when he was present.

It is usually very helpful to put yourself in another person's place when you feel resentful. You'll often realize that the other person is not trying to make your life miserable. Instead, just like you, he or she is trying to do what seems right at the time. Maybe you would make a different decision, but then you aren't that person. Most critically, though, empathy helps you become far less likely to build the kind of resentments that lead to seething rages.

STEP 6. *Consider four options to deal with lingering resentments and hate.*

What happens, though, if you don't cut off your resentments? Then these resentments gather power like a tropical storm in a warm sea, building up to hurricane strength. Eventually you can work yourself up until you feel total hatred toward another person. Hate is the end product of allowing your resentments to grow, when you won't or can't let go of them. In some ways, resentments are like anger that has become hardened or frozen. Once it gets that way, it just sits there like a rock. When you hate someone, all you can think about is how horrible he or she is. That person becomes a monster in your eyes. And, once you hate someone, you are far more likely to rage. Vinny, for instance, has become so hateful toward Charles that he is more than ready to attack him.

Hate is the fuel that energizes seething rage. So, if you are a seether, you need to find ways to let go of your hate.

How can you let go of hate? I believe there are four possible ways: distraction, emotional indifference, forgiveness, and reconciliation. Distraction is the simplest to achieve, although simple doesn't necessarily mean easy. None of these ways out of hate are easy at all. Hate is like the guest who comes to supper but then refuses to leave.

Distraction means making yourself do whatever you can to get on with your life. For Max, that meant getting a new job but staying in the field he loves, the organic food industry. When someone says they try to stay busy so they don't have to think of bad things, they are practicing distraction. The aim here is not to solve any problems or to reconnect with the hated person. It is simply to clear your mind as much as possible of useless obsession. Or, as is often said in Alcoholics Anonymous meetings, "Don't let someone have free rent in your brain." The idea is to start having fun again. You will know you are succeeding here when you notice that you are thinking a lot less than you used to about the person whom you have hated.

Emotional indifference means getting to a point where you can think about someone who has deeply offended you and you can do so without having extremely strong feelings. That person, along with the injuries he or she caused, becomes part of your past. Yes, it hurt at the time, but now it's over. There's no sense continuing to be miserable about what happened. The past cannot be changed, but it can be left behind. If Vinny can ever say that he is able to picture Charles and do so without immediately feeling a storm of emotion, he will have achieved a state of indifference.

You will know you have become emotionally indifferent toward someone you've hated when you can think about him or her without your stomach knotting up, your heart racing, or your voice rising. You may conclude that they are who they are, and so they, not you, will have to live with themselves.

The next two directions, forgiveness and reconciliation, are considerably more difficult to achieve than either distraction or emotional indifference. However, they may be more beneficial in the long run. Both forgiveness and reconciliation will help you heal the wounds from a broken relationship. They can also provide a great gift, the sense that life really can get better.

Perhaps the best definition of *forgiveness* I have found comes from psychoanalyst Robert Karen (2001): "Forgiveness is allowing someone back into your heart" (21). What he means is that forgiveness is an act of compassion and generosity toward someone who has harmed you. You are under no obligation to forgive (though some theologians disagree with this statement, since they believe that God wants and expects us to forgive). To insist you forgive only puts on extra pressure. However, forgiveness can be a tremendously healing experience. It is a transformative process, because when you forgive, you become a different person.

There is one catch to forgiving. You must be willing to give up your belief that the offender is completely bad and you are all good. Now it's easy to write down this idea on paper. But reality is different. You must deliberately choose to remember the good that the other person has done as well as the bad. For instance, when Max spends a little time reminiscing about the Three Brothers restaurant, he recalls that Charles was the guy who talked the other two into starting the business. "If Charles hadn't taken the initiative, I probably never would have realized how much I love organic foods. I'm grateful for that." Of course, Max still recognizes Charles's bad points. He isn't naïve. But he can balance those bad aspects with the good, and in doing so, he allows Charles back into his heart.

You will know that you have at least begun the forgiving process when you can hear others discussing the positive qualities of the person who offended you, and you can do so without having to jump in and start talking about his or her deficits. You'll be even further along when you can join in the conversation on the positive side.

Finally, *reconciliation* is the fourth possible way to let go of hate. To reconcile means to reconnect with the offender, to actually write or talk or have face-to-face contact with that person. Vinny, of course, believes that's impossible, that he could never trust Charles. Max, on the other hand, might be open to working with Charles again if he could become convinced that Charles's gambling problem was really over.

Reconciliation demands trust. You have to ask yourself why you think interacting with the offender will be different this time from previous times. Is there any evidence that the offender has changed? Is he or she doing things differently? If so, will these changes last? True reconciliation usually takes a long time. The offender basically has to prove (as much as anyone can prove their trustworthiness) that he or she can consistently behave in a respectful manner. While forgiving is something you do within yourself, reconciliation involves two or more people restoring a relationship.

You will be ready to reconcile with someone who has hurt you when you become convinced that the offender has changed enough so that he or she will not hurt or betray you. Also, you will probably only want to reconcile with someone when the good you see in him or her far outweighs any of his or her current bad, immature, or irresponsible behavior.

Do you need to let go of a feeling of hatred toward anyone? Would doing so help you quit seething? If so, think about these three questions:

1. "What new thoughts would help me be less hateful or rageful toward the person(s) who harmed me?"

2. "What was the person or people who harmed me thinking and feeling at the time of the offense? What were their motives other than just wanting to hurt me?"

3. "Which direction toward ending hate can I go toward: distraction, indifference, forgiveness, or reconciliation?"

Seething rage destroys your ability to enjoy life. Fortunately, it is possible to let go of old feelings of injury. That may be the only way to feel good about yourself, others, and the world.

Survival Rage

Terry: A Young Man Fighting for His Life

Terry is sixteen years old, the middle child of three boys. His father is a mean man who enjoys beating his children whenever he gets the notion. He's hardest on Terry, though, because he detects a kindness in his son that he considers a weakness. He tells Terry he hits him to toughen him up. Terry doesn't believe this for a minute, though. He knows that his father uses any excuse to attack. Terry keeps safe by staying away from his home as much as possible.

Terry can handle a regular beating. He can even handle what his dad calls "an old-fashioned whupping" with a belt buckle. But tonight his father has gone weird. He's been muttering to himself all day while drinking almost a whole case of beer. Now his father staggers into Terry's bedroom with an awful look on his face, a look that means he's planning on beating Terry until he gets too tired to raise his arm for another blow. Terry is trapped in his room, unable to run away.

That's when Terry snaps. He charges at his dad, screaming, "No, no, no, no, no!" He smashes into his father's chest, throwing him hard against the wall. He hears his dad shouting and swearing, threatening to kill him. And then Terry's mind goes blank. The next thing he becomes aware of is the weight of his two brothers, his mother, and two male neighbors holding him down. Next he sees his father, unconscious on the floor, a bloody, broken mess. "What happened?" he asks. George, his older brother, tells Terry that he kept screaming "no" all through the fight with his father. By the time George got there, Terry had knocked his father to the floor. But his dad got up and came back at Terry. So Terry slugged his father in the eye, dropping him again. He kicked him in the ribs several times and then right in the face. That's when his dad passed out, but even then, Terry kept screaming "no" and kicking. By then, his mother had run to the neighbors for help because Terry's two brothers couldn't stop him. "You were a madman, Terry. You just kept yelling and kicking. We couldn't pull you off Dad. We thought you were going to kill him."

Ten Years Later

Terry is twenty-six years old now. He's had several rage blackouts since that first one with his father. What bothers him is that they seem to be coming more frequently and with less provocation. Here's how Terry described his last rage: "It happened a couple weeks ago. I was at a party with two friends. I'd only had a couple beers. I wasn't drunk or even tipsy. I noticed a guy named Joey was watching me. He was looking at me funny, like he was sizing me up for a fight. I was scared but pissed off at the same time. I felt hot and cold, one right after the other, back and forth, hot and cold. Well, I wasn't going to wait for him to sneak up on me, so I walked over and challenged him. The next thing I knew, people were pulling me away. I lost about five minutes of time. They kicked me out of the party. My friends said I was cursing and yelling, screaming that I don't take shit from nobody. They said I threatened to kill that guy. They said, from the look in my eyes, that I wanted to kill him."

Terry doesn't know what's happening to him. He says he feels anxious a lot, but it's a funny kind of anxiety. "It's like there's always someone ready to attack me. I have to be on the defensive. I feel like a soldier on guard duty patrolling the perimeter of a territory. You never know when somebody will start shooting at you." Terry complains that he can't trust anyone. He feels alone and unsafe in a constantly threatening world. He just cannot break free from this feeling of impending danger. "The funny thing," Terry adds, "is actually I'm in no danger at all. My father hasn't touched me since that day in my bedroom. He wouldn't dare. And I live in a perfectly safe part of town. My girlfriend is sweet and gentle. She sees me go off and doesn't understand at all why I do that. I don't understand either. What's wrong with me?"

How Much Are You Like Terry?

How familiar are the two scenes above? Have you ever

- Gotten into a physical fight where you seemed to have incredible strength?

- Had a rage blackout, during which you said and did things you couldn't remember later?

- Threatened to severely hurt or even kill people you were angry with, even members of your family or others you love?

- Felt like you were fighting for your life when you got into an argument, even if only words were being exchanged?

- Become paranoid, thinking wrongly that people were out to get you?

- Had a fight-or-flight reaction, during which you felt both really angry and really scared?

■ Startled easily and strongly, for instance, when someone tapped you on the shoulder from behind?

If you are answering, "Yes, I do (or did) that," then chances are you have bouts of survival rage. Survival rage is a feeling of tremendous fury that is triggered by a real or imagined threat to a person's physical safety or survival.

Survival rages are primitive, basic, and fundamental to human existence. The message in a survival rage is simple: "You are threatening me. You could kill me. I must kill you first." Most people who experience survival rages have been threatened with death at some point in their lives, maybe when small and weak in childhood, perhaps in a gang as a teen or as a young soldier in wartime, possibly in a serious automobile or industrial accident, or even in a sexual assault or ongoing violent relationship. If you suffer from this rage, it means that something terrible happened to you, once or often; your survival rage is a response to the danger that you faced. Unfortunately, this way of reacting may outlive its original purpose. You rage when there is no real danger. You fight for your life when nobody is trying to kill you.

This chapter will describe how survival rages develop. But before going on, there is something important you need to think about if you are a survival rager. It's very easy to take on the role of victim when you have been abused. You can say, "Well, gee, it's not my fault I act crazy sometimes. After all, my dad [or mom or whoever else] abused me. He [she, they] ruined my life. I can't help it. That's just the way I am." So, instead of making a real commitment to gain control of your raging, you make excuses. All these excuses center on the theme of "I can't stop it. I can't control it. I can't change it. It's not my fault." Yes, it is not your fault. You didn't choose to be threatened with personal annihilation. You didn't volunteer to develop survival rage. But you can stop it. You can control it. You can change it. You can learn how to quit raging. If not, what's the point of reading this book?

Now I'm not saying it's easy to quit raging, especially survival raging. Far from it. But it is definitely possible to do so. To quit raging, you'll need to use all the tools in chapter 3 for gaining control over sudden rages, plus you'll want to study the guidelines for ending survival rages described later in this chapter.

The choice is simple. Either take control of your life, or let your survival raging run the show. Which do you want to happen?

How does someone take control, though? The first step is by gaining an understanding of how and why a particular behavior occurs. That's why the next topic here is a discussion of how people develop survival rages.

Terror and Trauma: The Roots of Survival Rage

Terry asks this question: "What's wrong with me?" Actually, there is a possible answer: "Terry, your brain may have been damaged by the abuse you suffered as a child." Scientists, in particular a man named Joseph LeDoux (1996, 2002), have been writing since the late 1990s about how terror and trauma affect people's brains. Here's a quick summary of their findings:

■ Emotions are absolutely critical to our existence as human beings. They provide important information that helps us survive. Our emotions tell us things like this: "Pay attention to this; it's really important," "Watch out, there's danger here," "Don't ever forget this or you could die," and, thankfully, "Hey, this is great. Let's keep doing it."

■ The brain has developed specific pathways to handle each emotion. These pathways are like highways that pass quickly through various parts of the brain. Most of these pathways are like city streets upon which traffic is pretty slow. But some pathways, the ones we use the most, are more like speedways where you can drive incredibly fast.

■ Now imagine that you see or sense something out of the corner of your eye that might be dangerous, perhaps a shadow on the wall or a person moving in your direction. Your brain instantly begins working, getting your body ready to fight or flee, if necessary. But this is not a time for leisurely thinking. If you are in real danger, you better get moving immediately. So the brain has developed a system to warn and prepare you that works almost instantly. Within about a quarter of a second, messengers begin racing through the brain, quickly reaching a little almond-shaped place called the amygdala. The amygdala is your emotional warning center. Its job is to yell out "Danger, danger, danger!" within your brain and body. When the amygdala is doing that job, you'll instantly freeze for a moment to figure out where the danger is located. Meanwhile, the amygdala signals your adrenal gland to begin pumping the stress hormone cortisol into your body so that you can fight for your life in case that shadowy figure coming your way is an enemy.

■ But wait! What if that's not an enemy? What if it's only friendly Uncle Joe coming to say hello. You really don't want to shoot him first and ask questions later, do you? So our brains have a second pathway, one that goes through more sophisticated parts of the brain—places where things can be put into perspective. That system allows you to think, "Wait a second. That's Uncle Joe. I don't have to be scared." However, it takes longer, at least a couple seconds, for the amygdala to receive this message.

■ There's one other part of the brain that's very important to name and discuss. That is a body called the *hippocampus*, which sits virtually right next to the amygdala. The hippocampus helps people remember past emotional events and put things into proper perspective. Most importantly, it signals the adrenal gland to quit pumping out cortisol if there is no real danger.

■ Normally, there is a delicate balance between the amygdala telling the adrenal gland to deliver cortisol and the hippocampus signaling it to stop. Imagine two people inside your head, side by side, one a worrywart and one totally calm but maybe a little too trusting. The amygdala is the worrywart. It's always saying, "Watch out! Danger! Run! Fight! Do something!" Meanwhile, the hippocampus is going, "Oh, no, no, no. Relax. Everything's cool. We're in no danger." The normal result is very healthy: when there is real danger, the amygdala stays in control to help you survive. But when the danger turns out to be a false alarm (which is almost all the time), then the hippocampus can take over and end the crisis.

■ Now comes the bad part if you've ever been terribly threatened: trauma can destroy this fragile balance between excitement and calmness. One way this happens is that during periods of grave danger, the adrenal gland can deliver so much cortisol that the hippocampus gets seriously damaged. As a result, the hippocampus no longer can keep pace with the amygdala when it tells the adrenal gland to produce more cortisol. It's as if the amygdala shouts "More cortisol!" while the hippocampus can only whisper "Less, please." The hippocampus gradually becomes smaller and less effective, sometimes shrinking by as much as one-sixth of its normal size.

■ What all this means is that people like Terry come to live in a state of perpetual agitation. Their brains regularly misinterpret situations, finding danger in every nook and cranny of human existence. That shadowy figure must be an enemy. That dinner invitation must be a trap. That stick must really be a snake. Terry's traumatized and damaged brain gives him seriously distorted information about the world. His emotional state becomes one of fearful guardedness. Terry cannot rest. He cannot relax. Terry's brain, like that of many traumatized people, has been redesigned to help him survive in a constantly threatening world.

From Flight to Fight

Terry's constant wariness sets the stage for what scientists call *defensive aggression*. The message here is "I am in danger. I have to fight." Remember that Terry only challenged the stranger at the party because he thought that man had "looked at me funny." This kind of statement is common among people with traumatized brains who are oversensitized to danger. Of course, there was no real proof that the guy at the party was looking for a fight. No matter, though. Terry was certain enough that he immediately attacked this newfound enemy.

Defensive aggression is, like fear, a reaction to threat. Instead of running away, the threatened person turns on the attacker, often hoping to scare off him or her, or at least get in the first blow. Terry turns flight into fight as fear gives way to anger. He feels safer and stronger getting angry than he does feeling scared. Besides, Terry's probably been taught, like most men, to believe that males should never give in to their fears. He'll try to show his anger, not his fear, to the other guy, by moving closer, glaring, raising his voice, and making threatening remarks. Sometimes this works. The opponent backs away. But sometimes these behaviors trigger other people's anger and defensive aggression, resulting in useless pissing contests, shoving bouts, or far worse.

False Alarms, the Slide from Reality, and Survival Rages

Does Terry seem a little paranoid to you? He is indeed paranoid, maybe not enough to convince a psychiatrist that he needs medications, but more than enough to get him into trouble. Terry consistently misinterprets reality. More specifically, he sees danger where there is no danger, even threats to his existence where there are no threats.

Here's the problem. Terry's survival-oriented brain is programmed to search continually for any hints of trouble. If there are any small signs (such as a guy looking in his direction), he exaggerates and distorts them, so they seem much worse than they really are. If there aren't any danger signs, Terry's brain may simply create them. Terry's brain keeps giving him false alarm signals.

Unfortunately, Terry isn't getting better. In fact, he is getting worse over time. That's because every false alarm triggers the release of more cortisol, more adrenaline, more of everything the body uses to battle danger. These chemicals keep eating away at Terry's amygdala and hippocampus, corrupting the entire system. It's as if Terry were on a slide that keeps moving him farther and farther away from good judgment.

Can you see where this is going? Terry is becoming more irrational. He cannot distinguish real danger from imaginary danger. He overreacts to perceived threats. Each time he does so, he loses more control over his emotional and physical reactions. Terry is heading right toward rage. Specifically, Terry is likely to begin having *false survival rages*. These false survival rages look and feel the same as real survival rages to the rager. The only difference is this: there is legitimate life-threatening danger during a real survival rage while there is no real danger during a false survival rage.

Survival Rages as Fight-or-Flight Reactions

Anger and fear are closely related emotions. For instance, they both travel through the amygdala in the brain. They need to be closely connected in our brains because people often have to decide quickly between standing their ground or running away in the face of immediate danger. That's the classic fight-or-flight choice. However, people like Terry seem to have a strong fight *and* flight reaction when raging.

Imagine you are one of a small group of soldiers conducting a search for enemy troops. You're expecting to run into a few of the enemy at a time. Instead, though, you stumble across a much larger unit. The enemy greatly outnumbers you. So now, what do you do? You must shoot and run at the same time. That's the only way to survive. And what are you feeling? Both anger and fear. Your anger helps you fire at the enemy. Your fear helps you escape.

I believe that survival rages are usually triggered by mixed (and very strong) fear and anger. It's the combination of these two emotions that overwhelms reason. True, when someone is raging, all you can see is the anger. But remember the core message: "I've got to kill you before you kill me." That's very different from "I want to kill you to get what I want" or "I want to kill you to get you out of my way." It's the fear of death that directs the attack.

Why is this so important? It means that Terry, or anyone else trying to control this kind of raging, must deal with his or her fear as well as his or her anger. It means that feeling safer is the key to rage control. So we're not just talking about anger management here. We're talking about helping people change how they relate to the world.

Now here's the dilemma. Traumatized people see danger everywhere, anywhere, with everyone. There is no safe place. There are no safe people. Most importantly, they often see danger when there is no danger. So how can Terry (and maybe you, the reader) quit having survival rages? The answer, obviously, is that Terry must retrain his brain. He must convince himself that he lives in a safe enough world, so he can quit shooting and running. Note the words "safe enough"—not perfectly safe. None of us live in a perfectly safe world. A safe enough world is one in which you feel no immediate danger to your life and well-being. A safe enough world is also one in which you believe that most people, especially those closest to you, are on your side and want to protect rather than harm you.

Stopping Survival Rages

Here are four steps that you must take to stop having survival rages.

STEP 1. *Learn to question your sense of how much danger you are really in at any time.*

People always want to believe their brains give them perfectly accurate information about the world. But what if that's not true? What if your brain consistently gives you false, exaggerated, or distorted information? Once you figured that out, wouldn't you want to do things very differently? Well, that's exactly the situation for people like Terry who have frequent survival rages. Their brains keep telling them they are in far more danger than they actually are.

Debra Niehoff (1998), a scientist studying anger and violence, writes that "the key to tempering violent behavior is adjusting the … [sensed] threat so that the intensity of the response matches the true demands of the situation" (264). What she's saying is that our brains need to work well enough to distinguish accurately between situations that pose no threat and those that pose little danger, great danger, or are life-threatening. But that's just what trauma survivors have trouble doing. They make the same mistake over and over again, wrongly believing they are in danger. Their misinterpretations of reality trigger false (unnecessary) survival rages.

If you have these useless and dangerous survival rages, then you must learn to question the accuracy of your perceptions and interpretations of reality. You have to treat your brain as if you were a well-trained detective listening to a somewhat dubious story, like the following:

Your Brain:	"Honest, officer, that guy at the party is threatening me."
Detective:	"Sure, sure, that's what you always say. Where's your proof?"
Your Brain:	"Well, he's looking at me kind of funny."
Detective:	"Oh, come on. He's just glancing all around the room like people do at parties."
Your Brain:	"But he has a mean look, just like my father had."

Detective:	"That's because he's wearing a mustache like your father. You can't go bashing him just because he has a mustache."
Your Brain:	"You really think he's okay?"
Detective:	"Look, he doesn't know you from Adam. He's just a guy at a party. He's not out to get you. Relax."
Your Brain:	"Okay, I'll try."

Here's my point: if you've had survival rages, don't trust your brain to give you accurate information in the area of threat assessment. That brain of yours may work fine everywhere else, but it makes a lot of mistakes when watching for danger signs. You must seriously check things out when you feel threatened. But be careful here, too. Checking things out does not mean looking only for signs or hints or clues that confirm your worst fears. You must actively look for things that can help you feel safe around others.

It often helps to have a couple of friends around who can help you stay in reality. That detective inside you needs allies. Take the following example:

You:	"Al, can I talk to you for a minute? You see that guy over there? I think he's looking funny at me."
Al:	"Hey, pal, don't get crazy. I know that guy. He's okay."

STEP 2. *Memorize a few brief sayings that you can repeat to yourself immediately when you first feel threatened. Then practice them religiously.*

Helene, fifty, grew up poor. She has worried about money all her life. But one day she discovered a one-word thought that has helped her immensely. Now, when she begins worrying about how much money she has or needs, Helene says that one word to herself and feels immediate relief: "Enough." That's the word, as in "I have enough money."

That's exactly the kind of thought Terry needs to stop raging. Not that specific word, of course, but some word or saying that he can say to himself quickly when he feels threatened. Terry will need a word or phrase that meets these tests:

1. It has to be simple.

2. It has to feel right.

3. It has to help him stay calm.

4. It has to stop the rage in its tracks.

Remember that our brains react to sensed danger almost instantly, within less than a second. Probably nobody can stop that initial startle reaction. But within a couple seconds, we begin getting better, more complete information that usually helps us calm down. Our frontal lobes kick in, as well as the hippocampus, putting things into better perspective. However, that tiny time gap makes some people vulnerable to survival rages, especially if their brains have been damaged by trauma. The idea here is to form a mental and emotional bridge between those two pathways. You need to immediately challenge that initial feeling of danger.

I believe almost every survival rager can find a phrase or thought that can really help him or her stay calm. However, every person is unique. That means the phrase Terry or someone else uses might not help you. The challenge for you, if indeed you rage like this, is to find the one or two magic phrases that actually work for you.

Here are several possibilities:

"Slow down."

"I'm safe."

"No danger."

"Stay calm."

"Trust God."

"Think."

"Breathe."

"No enemies today."

"Relax."

"No false alarms."

"Don't get paranoid."

"Easy does it."

Nothing fancy. Nothing complex. These phrases go immediately to your brain's emotional center. So what phrases could you use to help you quit raging?

One more thing. It's no good choosing a phrase unless you use it regularly. Don't wait until that guy at the party looks at you funny. Instead, begin each day thinking your phrase. For instance, think "no enemies today" every morning as you shower or look in the mirror. Bring that phrase into your brain, your heart, your soul. Make it part of your life.

STEP 3. *Surround yourself with safe people.*

So far, this chapter has made one assumption. It is that you, the reader, live in a reasonably safe situation. But what if that isn't true? What if you are living with a battering spouse who might beat you at any time? What if you live in an exceedingly dangerous neighborhood in the middle of a cocaine and methamphetamine district? What if you belong to a gang in which violence is considered normal and routine? What if you regularly hang out at a tavern where some rowdies are always picking fights? What if you are right now a member of the armed forces on active duty in a country seething with enemies? What if you are a teen living at home with a sexually or physically abusive parent or sibling? What if you are a prisoner at a high-risk penal institution surrounded by people who would kill you in a heartbeat?

How could anyone expect you to gain control over your survival rages under those circumstances? After all, you might need one to survive. On the other hand, though, maybe that's the last thing you need to do when the situation is dangerous. It might be better to be able to think, plan, and escape the danger rather than attack it.

The best thing you can do, naturally, is to get out of these bad situations. Leave your battering spouse—nobody deserves to get beaten. Drop out of the gang. Choose to live with your mother if your father beats you, or find another family if both parents are at fault. Do your time well, so you can get an early release. Move out of that crappy neighborhood, even if it means having to get a second job. Find a new bar to hang out in, or quit drinking. Remember that safety comes first. Safety means everything. Feeling safe makes it much easier to quit raging.

But maybe that's not possible. You're on active duty for a year. You don't have the money to move. The courts have ordered you to stay with your father. You still love your spouse too much to leave. You're stuck in that prison for another five years. You face danger every day. Still, there is something you can do. In fact, you may need to do this to survive. Find safe people. Surround yourself with them, so you can feel as safe as possible even in difficult situations.

What makes someone safe? First, remember that the best predictor of future behavior is past behavior. So the safest people have a good track record of never hitting or hurting you. Nor do they hit or hurt others. Secondly, safe people protect you from danger when they can. They warn you away from trouble. They guard your back when needed. They try to help you stay safe. Next, these people consistently match their words with their actions. That means they are reliable. They don't say they are on your side but act as if they were your enemy. Fourthly, safe people care about you, think about you, ask about you, and want to help you when they can. They truly want you to have a good life. Finally, you usually will feel safe with safe people. Maybe not at first, but eventually, as they gain your trust over time.

So find those safe people. Hang out with them as often as you can. Learn from them what it feels like to feel safe inside. Maybe, eventually, you can help them feel safer too.

STEP 4. *Consider getting help to specifically address your traumatic history and to help you separate the past from the present.*

Terry's been dating a great woman named Marcie. She's thoughtful, caring, a wonderful listener. One day, Marcie says to him, "Terry, tell me your story." Terry would love to do that. He needs her to understand how badly wounding his childhood was. Still, he hesitates at first, afraid that talking about his demons will only make them worse. But Marcie encourages him to talk, because she really wants to learn all about him.

Initially everything goes well. Terry tells Marcie about how poor his family was, how they barely had enough to eat. Then he decides to take a chance and tell her about the beatings he received from his father. And that's when the bad stuff starts. He can feel himself sliding into his past. He goes from remembering his dad coming to beat him to being right there in the bedroom again, terrified and enraged. Terry's eyes narrow into a glare, but he isn't seeing anything real. His whole body begins trembling. Terry begins saying "no, no, no," just like he did that day he had his first survival rage. Marcie soon realizes he's in trouble. She tries to help Terry by shaking his shoulders to get him back to the present. That's when he swings, knocking her to the ground. Later, he'll tell her he didn't recognize her. Terry thought he was punching his father, not Marcie. He felt he was fighting for his life all over again. It takes him fifteen minutes to snap out of the past and several hours before he can calm down.

Traumatized people sometimes get trapped in their pasts. It's like they're getting pulled into the black hole of their memories from which they'll never be able to escape. Their past becomes their present. That's when grown men or women become scared and desperate children. They feel now what they felt back then. They think now the way they thought at the time.

It's difficult to act rationally when you are stuck in the past. It's awfully hard to quit raging when you feel totally threatened. That's why I strongly recommend you seek out people who can help you deal with your past traumas, especially if you have dissociative experiences like I've just described. Fortunately, there are people who can help you. Some of them may be good friends, teachers, ministers, or family members—people with big hearts, good ears, common sense, and lots of patience. Also consider trying professional therapy. These days, many therapists specialize in trauma work. They have specific training in helping clients work through their past wounds without becoming retraumatized in the process. One advantage of working with a professional is that you won't have to worry about saying or doing something that might hurt the people you love. You won't have to protect your therapist from yourself.

Whether you are talking with friends or a therapist, the goal is to separate your past from the present as a way to stop having unnecessary survival rages.

Survival rages are powerful, primitive, and dangerous. They come on fast and fierce. Nevertheless, you can manage to gain control over them. You don't have to let them ruin your life.

6

Impotent Rage

Carlene: A Woman Who Feels Helpless, Trapped, and Angry

Carlene, forty, divorced her husband of fifteen years for one main reason: "Clark was so controlling. He wanted to run every aspect of my life. I couldn't breathe." Unfortunately, though, Clark is still in her life because of their two children, for whom they share custody and living arrangements. And he's still trying to control Carlene. Clark calls constantly when she has the kids, telling her how to handle them. He gets mean, too, if she doesn't do things his way. He swears at her while accusing her of being a "pathetic" mother.

Clark plays mind games that seem designed to get under Carlene's skin. Just the other day, he promised to pick the kids up from their soccer practice but then didn't show up. That meant Carlene had to leave work early to get them. When she complained to Clark, he just laughed at her. He also tries to turn the children against Carlene; he buys them things she can't afford and tells them that Carlene's the cause of their divorce. He's not above guilt-tripping, either, telling Carlene that she ruined the kids' lives by destroying the family.

Carlene knows she should just shrug off Clark's dumb games, nasty mouth, obvious manipulations, and guilt-trips. She wishes she could. But instead, she finds herself obsessing about him. "What will he do next? Why is he doing this to me? Why won't he stop?" She's thinking more about him now than when they were married. But here's the worst part. Carlene feels she is still under Clark's control. She can't breathe. She feels helpless, unable to set and maintain a boundary between herself and her ex. But watch out. Carlene's getting madder and madder all the time.

Carlene Raging

Carlene gets angry a lot with Clark. Every so often, she yells at him to just leave her alone. But these are little blasts, like steam coming from the vents of a slumbering volcano. Then she receives a registered letter, informing her that Clark is taking her back to court to try to make her pay child support. Clark's reason: he kept the kids one day more than she did the last calendar year. So that's why he offered so generously for them to sleep over on New Year's Eve! And here comes Clark right this minute sauntering up the driveway as if nothing were going on.

Carlene goes crazy mad. She screams and screams. She rips up the notice and throws it in his face. She pushes his chest as hard as she can, forcing him to give ground even though he weighs over 200 pounds. Carlene hears herself saying things she's never said before, swearing at the top of her lungs. The more she shouts, the more she wants to shout. When Clark tries to get into his car to leave, she hops in the other side and keeps ranting. She's so furious, she's spitting as she talks. Nor will she stop. She goes on like this for over half an hour. Periodically, she slows down for a few seconds, but then she starts yelling again. She's become a volcano in full eruption, a Mt. Vesuvius of anger. Carlene is raging.

Notice, however, that Carlene's rage differs from Terry's survival rage described in chapter 5. For instance, Carlene hasn't lost consciousness. Most importantly, the fuel for Carlene's rage is her sense of utter frustration and powerlessness, not a fear of death. What Carlene is experiencing is impotent rage.

Impotent Rage

Impotent rage is a feeling of tremendous fury that is triggered by the sense of helplessness that occurs when a person is unable to control important situations. It can happen after somebody does everything possible to alter an important situation, but nothing works. For example, Myron has been battling his cancer for several years. Myron felt impotent rage after trying prayer, chemotherapy, radiation, alternative medications, and even experimental drugs, only to find nothing slowed down the disease. He ended up literally shaking his fist at God, demanding to know why he was being tortured this way. When God didn't answer, Myron felt even more helpless fury. He was rageful at himself, God, his family, and the world.

Impotent rages usually build slowly. People simmer, seethe, stew, and smolder. They try one thing after another to make things better. But nothing works for long. Often, life gets worse instead of better. Carlene feels more and more trapped. Myron gets sicker and sicker. They keep trying. They dig in deeper. But the pain simply will not go away. Finally, the pressure builds until they blow.

What About You?

Before continuing, think of a situation you've had in which you felt helpless and out of control. Which of the questions below would help describe how you felt at the time?

- Did you feel like exploding because people didn't seem to be listening to you or understanding you?

- Did you feel both helpless and furious about a situation that you couldn't control?

- Did you say to yourself, "I just can't take it anymore," or have similar thoughts?

- Did you get so angry that you had to do something— anything—even if it made the problem worse?

- Did you pound the ground, break things, or scream out loud when things didn't go the way you wanted them to?

- Did you harbor thoughts of violence or revenge toward people who had power or control over you?

- Did you lose control, saying and doing things you later regretted?

- Did you find yourself violently raging against people and situations you couldn't control?

- What about now? Are you having those same thoughts and feelings? How close are you to going through an impotent rage today?

The Key to Understanding Impotent Rage

What happens to people that leads them to rage like this? Actually, one simple idea is at the center of all impotent rages: anger develops whenever people feel out of control of their own fate. This is particularly true for Americans and people from other Western countries that stress independence, self-determination, privacy, and self-control. We are expected to be masters of our own fate. To be independent is strong. To be dependent upon others is weak. To be in charge of your own life is powerful. To be in the hands of others is pitiful.

What happens when people lose control of their lives? You can go to your average nursing home for an answer. That's where you'll find some angry, bitter older men and women. They're furious with a world in which they no longer can decide when to get up in the morning, what to eat, and with whom to talk. "Go away, leave me alone" is their theme. Their freedom has been restricted, and they don't appreciate it one bit.

People of any age protest against the loss of free choice. They fight back. But sometimes they lose ground, no matter how hard they fight. They may become desperate. That's when impotent rages develop.

Here's an example from the movies. In the film *John Q.*, Denzel Washington plays a quiet, gentle, average man, somebody blown around rather helplessly by the layoffs and cutbacks at his factory. He's not a guy who takes a strong stand on anything. He just wants to get by and have a good life. Then his son almost dies suddenly from heart failure. John Q.'s son needs a heart transplant to survive. But John Q. doesn't have enough insurance. His son is dying as he stands by helplessly. He tries talking reasonably with the hospital's financial director. That's useless. He tries to borrow the money. No luck. His son is getting sicker and sicker. John's wife screams at him, "John, do something!" His response: John Q. goes home, packs a gun, and takes over the emergency room of the hospital. He doesn't have a plan. He's not sure how this will help. But John Q. feels that he has to do something, anything, to save his son's life.

It takes a lot of misery to produce an impotent rage. The key is that you gradually feel more and more desperate as you struggle ineffectively to control your own fate.

The Six Main Components of Impotent Rage

There are six separate components of impotent rage, each of which is like a storm-filled stream. When all of those streams pour their waters into a river, it may jump its banks. That's when people think, "I can't take it anymore," and go off on a rage.

How familiar are you with these components of impotent rage?

1. Ragers believe they have been seriously injured by others. These injuries may be physical, financial, or emotional.

2. Ragers feel helpless to change the situation after they've made repeated efforts.

3. Ragers eventually run out of socially acceptable ways to address the issue.

4. Ragers become obsessed with the problem, virtually unable to think about anything else.

5. Ragers increasingly see themselves as innocent victims of others' thoughtless or intentional actions against them. They begin to think of their adversaries as evil people who must be punished.

6. Ragers then plan and sometimes carry out specific actions designed at least symbolically to right the wrongs they have suffered.

Let's take a good look at each of these impotent rage components. To put the meat of real experience on the bones of theory, though, here's a true story of a man whose helpless fury led to a fatal assault.

Bart Ross, Impotent Rager

February 28, 2005. A man named Bart Ross breaks into the Chicago home of Judge Joan Lefkow. He lurks there for several hours. He plans to kill Judge Lefkow. Instead, Ross is discovered by her husband and mother. He shoots both of them dead, then leaves the house. He soon kills himself as well, leaving behind a suicide note detailing his wrath.

I believe Bart Ross provides an excellent example of how impotent rages develop. He appears to have gone through each of the six steps just mentioned.

STEP 1. *He believed he had been seriously injured, not just once but many times.*

Bart Ross had been treated for mouth cancer at a Chicago hospital in the mid-1990s. He believed the operation had been botched, causing him to be disfigured. In his mind, that was the first injustice. But then came many more. He tried to sue the hospital and doctors involved but never won anything. His case got thrown out of several courts. Finally, he sued in federal court, seeking millions of dollars from the state of Illinois, doctors, and attorneys. Judge Lefkow was in charge of that case.

Notice that reality is not the issue here. Perhaps Ross was entirely delusional. Maybe there was a grain of truth in his arguments. What matters is that he was absolutely certain he was right. He was convinced he had been grievously injured over and over by a heartless and thoughtless social system. That belief is what propelled him into action.

STEP 2. *Ross felt helpless to change the situation after he'd made repeated efforts.*

Ross wrote in his suicide note that "lawyers are telling me to get a doctor and doctors are telling me to get a lawyer" (Slevin 2005, 11A). He claimed to have driven over 5,000 miles and contacted hundreds of attorneys and physicians in his efforts. All of this work was to no avail, however. He was no closer to getting what he considered to be justice in 2005 than he was ten years earlier.

Here are some words that describe the feelings of people at this stage: helpless, overwhelmed, outmaneuvered, weak, desperate, misunderstood, ganged up on, scapegoated, and abandoned. Nevertheless, the human need to fix problems may keep people going, even in the face of overwhelming failure. The word that Ross probably could not bear was "defeated." He continued to plead his case.

STEP 3. Ross eventually ran out of socially acceptable ways to address the issue.

At some point, people heading for an impotent rage run out of socially acceptable options. Nobody would take Ross's case. Nobody would fight for him. Of course, most people would have given up the battle much earlier. These people would want to get on with their lives, even though they felt they had been badly hurt. If Ross had been able to do that, three people would probably still be alive today. But he could not let go. Out of socially acceptable options, he began thinking about far more aggressive possibilities.

STEP 4. Ross became obsessed with the problem, virtually unable to think about anything else.

As pressure builds, the world of ragers becomes psychologically smaller and smaller. Their injuries are all they can think about. The meaning of their lives becomes focused upon redressing their wounds. They become totally obsessed. Eventually, they become masters at steering conversations toward the one and only thing that matters in their lives. For instance, a discussion about tomatoes could lead a man like Bart Ross to complain that he can't eat tomatoes now because of what the doctors did to his mouth.

STEP 5. Ross increasingly saw himself as an innocent victim of actions against him.

Paranoia is a close cousin of obsession. The more you obsess, the easier it is to become convinced that people are out to get you. Everyone who doesn't take your side becomes an enemy. Ross, like all paranoids, thought of himself as an innocent victim of the evil intent of others. Ross wrote in one letter that Judge Lefkow was a "Nazi-style criminal and terrorist" who used outrageous judicial power to harm him (Slevin 2005, 11A).

STEP 6. *Ross then planned and carried out specific actions designed to right the wrongs he had suffered.*

Bart Ross believed that he and only he was a victim here. He also apparently believed that he had a right to seek revenge against those people who had harmed him. Who knows how long it took him to come up with his plan? He went on a rampage designed to attack not just one particular judge but the entire medical/judicial system. Ross wanted and needed to do something that would say to the world and to himself that he was no longer a weak, helpless victim.

Thankfully, there are few Bart Rosses in the world. But many, many people do simmer with rage against those they believe have harmed them. They may occasionally lose at least partial control. You, the reader, may be one of these people. If so, please pay special attention to the rest of this chapter.

How to Prevent Impotent Rages

Impotent rages occur when people believe they have lost control over their own lives. The key to prevention, then, is to find ways to regain a sense of personal control. There are two main ways to regain that sense of control:

1. Figure out some new, more effective actions to take.

2. Accept reality, let go of a hopeless fight, and get on with your life.

Some situations call for the first solution, some for the second, and many situations are best handled using a combination of these approaches. I will describe both ways to prevent impotent rage below. First, though, ask yourself if you have any situations in which your anger has been building toward helpless fury. The situation may be as small as your paper getting delivered late most every day, or it may be a much more serious issue, like Carlene's running battle with her former husband. Consider what approach might be most helpful as you read the next few pages.

Figure Out More Effective Actions

You may be familiar with the old saying "if it ain't broke, don't fix it." Well, think about the flip side of that idea: "If it ain't working, do something different." That's one key to preventing impotent rage.

Here are the six steps you'll need to take in order to take new actions.

STEP 1. Analyze what's going wrong.

After her rage at Clark, Carlene took stock of her situation. She realized that she kept setting herself up to be furious with him. "I keep thinking he'll be fair and reasonable with me. I convince myself he'll put the kids' best interest ahead of his own. I expect him to be thoughtful, caring, and considerate." The trouble is that Clark has never been thoughtful, caring, and considerate. In fact, Carlene divorced him mostly because he was almost always thoughtless, mean, and inconsiderate. So why would she expect him to change now?

Carlene, like most people, tends to repeat her mistakes. She does the same thing over and over, expecting different results. In this case, she asks Clark to do something nice, or she expects him to keep his promises. That puts her well-being into Clark's hands. That's not smart. He then fails to meet her expectations. And that's when Carlene becomes totally frustrated. She feels weak, stupid, and very, very angry every time this happens. No wonder she finally had a meltdown.

Are you doing the same thing as Carlene? Are you expecting new results from old, ineffective behavior? If so, you too are setting yourself up for an impotent rage.

STEP 2. Quit doing what isn't working.

It's seldom easy to change old behavior. But Carlene knows she must do so in order to quit raging at Clark. So she sits down and makes a "Don't Do These Things" list. Don't ask Clark for anything. Don't count on him ever being on time. Don't expect him to keep his promises. Don't do him any favors, no matter how sweetly he asks. Don't help him out when it's his time with the kids. Don't depend on Clark for anything. None of these behaviors has gotten her what she wanted. Each of them has only fueled her anger.

How about you? What are you doing that isn't working? What specific behaviors do you need to stop?

STEP 3. *Develop new, realistic goals.*

One key to preventing impotent rage is to take effective action. It won't be enough for Carlene just to quit doing what she's been doing. She'll just create an emotional vacuum that way. Carlene must come up with a new game plan. That means setting realistic goals.

Carlene comes up with this general goal: to maximize her control of situations in which she interacts with Clark. She knows it's a good goal, because she can feel herself relaxing just by picturing it in her mind. Carlene sets this goal to give direction to how she deals with Clark. She also realizes that it won't be an easy goal to achieve. Clark has been getting his way for a long time and won't give up power willingly. But setting this positive goal helps Carlene remember that she, not Clark, is in control of her life.

What general goal do you need to set in your frustrating situation? Can you come up with a goal that helps you feel more in control of your own life?

STEP 4. *Design specific plans to reach your goals.*

Carlene's next step is to turn her general goal into a specific plan of action. That calls for a lot of thought. No fuzzy wishes allowed. She needs clear guidelines. Carlene needs a specific "do" list to complement the "don't" list she already composed. Here's what she decides: Do keep records of every time Clark shows up late with the kids. Do tell him exactly what she will and won't do in any situation. Do insist upon specific and exact commitments from Clark whenever he makes a promise to do something. Do hire an attorney if Clark persists in trying to make her pay child support. Do only what she's supposed to do with the kids, no matter what excuses he comes up with.

Carlene may have to add to this list over time. But for now, this list of dos, along with the don'ts, provides clear guidelines for new behavior.

Now it's your turn. Can you design a list of at least a half dozen "dos" that will help you feel stronger and more effective? Doing so will really help you feel less frustrated and angry.

STEP 5. *Try out these new behaviors.*

New behavior is hard to begin and harder yet to keep doing. Fortunately, though, Clark gives Carlene many opportunities for practice. Just yesterday, for instance, he called and asked her if she would take the kids back a couple days early from his scheduled week with them. Carlene would always have done so in the past. But after saying okay, she always felt used and suckered. So this time, she says no. Of course, Clark gets upset. First, he tries to guilt-trip her into taking them. When that doesn't work, he threatens to get back at her the next time she asks him for a favor. But that's not a problem because Carlene hasn't asked him for anything since she composed her "don't" list. Instead of wavering and eventually giving in, Carlene stands firm. Furthermore, she informs Clark that he must drop the children off between 6 and 8 P.M. Friday night, as written in the court order, not earlier in the day. Clark grumbles again and hangs up abruptly. But chances are good he'll obey the court order. Besides, Carlene has made plans for Friday. She won't even be home until just before 6 P.M., so he can't drop the kids off early. A little to her surprise, Carlene's new behaviors are working.

What new behavior would you select to try out in the immediate future to help remedy your frustrating situation? If it works, will you keep doing it? If it doesn't work, will you be able to figure out what went wrong?

STEP 6. *Regularly review your progress and be prepared to keep experimenting if necessary.*

Carlene's getting better. She no longer simmers with anger every time she thinks of Clark. She stays pretty calm around him, too. But she is still frustrated by one of his antics. Clark keeps buying the children clothes they don't need. Fancy coats. Expensive accessories. Delicate articles that need special care. The kids don't even want that stuff. In fact, he insists they wear these clothes when he drops them off at Carlene's house. She realizes he's doing it to put her down, to boast about having more money than she does.

Carlene's new strategy: she informs Clark that she will no longer wash, mend, or handle these new clothes. Instead, she will simply bag them when the kids wear them to her house. He can wash them himself. Sure enough, Clark soon quits making the children wear those clothes home.

Nothing works forever. So be prepared to design and develop new strategies to replace ones that no longer work. You'll need to do something different if you find yourself once again building up toward an impotent rage.

Accept Reality

There have been many books written on living with troublesome, irritating, and difficult people. But no matter what you say or do, these people usually remain troublesome, irritating, and difficult. Carlene's ex-husband, Clark, for instance, drags her down with his endless complaining and lecturing, no matter what she does. She feels like strangling him every time he calls. Carlene doesn't want to have another impotent rage. It took her weeks to get over that last one. But she can feel herself working up to one.

So now what? Carlene needs to redirect her energy away from Clark and toward herself. She's got to accept reality (Clark isn't going to change), quit trying to control him, and get on with her life.

Here are the six steps Carlene must take. They will help you, too, if you need to let go of a hopeless fight in order to gain back control of your life.

STEP 1. *First, you must recognize the limits of your control over the universe.*

You've probably said the serenity prayer, in one form or another, many times in your life. "God grant me the serenity to change the things I can, accept the things I cannot change, and the wisdom to know the difference." Well, I believe the hardest part of this prayer is the second—to accept the things we cannot change. We human beings just aren't very good at accepting limits on what we can do.

If you are susceptible to impotent rages, you probably are very persistent. You don't give up easily. You keep fighting for what you think is morally right or absolutely necessary. This persistence is a virtue in many areas. For example, you probably are really good at finishing whatever tasks you begin. However, a person's strength can become a weakness. You may not be able to accept the reality that what you want to change cannot be controlled.

Some people don't change. That's just the way it is. Some things cannot be controlled, no matter how much time and effort you put into them. Have you been clinging to the illusion of control? If so, why?

Ask yourself this question: What is hard for you to accept about not being in total control of your world? Is it the fear that something terrible will happen? Or that someone else will take over your life and control you? That you will feel weak and small? That you will die?

Now try out this statement: "I accept the reality that I have limited power and control over the universe." How does that feel?

How about this one? "I accept the reality that I cannot control _____." Please fill in the blank with the name of someone you have been trying unsuccessfully to control.

STEP 2. *Be specific about exactly what you cannot control in any particular situation.*

Accepting your limited power in the universe is absolutely necessary to prevent impotent rage. But a general philosophical statement isn't enough. You need to get down to specifics. That means Carlene must remind herself regularly that she cannot control Clark. But she still needs to become more concrete in her thinking. At the next layer down, she has to remind herself that she cannot control his game playing, manipulations, and cons. Finally, she needs to recognize that she cannot control the time he brings the children home, the things he says to them during their stays with him, or whether or not he'll take her back to court.

Accepting your limited control is like paddling a canoe upstream. Resistance is inevitable. So Carlene will have to do more than just think these thoughts once in a while. She'll need to remind herself each and every time Clark picks up the kids that she has to let go of trying to control the situation. She'll probably need support from others as well—a caring friend who has gone through the same stuff, a loving parent, a divorce survival group, or a counselor. These people can help her get that canoe to safety.

Please fill in the blanks in the following statements to say exactly what you cannot control in a specific situation that could lead you toward impotent rage.

"I must accept the fact that I cannot control _____."

"I also cannot control _____."

"And I can't control _____."

STEP 3. *Ask yourself what you have been wanting from someone that you will never get.*

So far, we've been looking directly at immediate issues. But impotent rages are powerful and tenacious. They develop in the depths of your soul. They revolve around your most significant wants and needs. You can't prevent an impotent rage simply by thinking a few sensible thoughts. It's important to look deeper inside.

A deep-seated wish, a frustrated yearning, frequently lies at the heart of an impotent rage. Carlene finally recognized that all along she'd been hoping Clark would appreciate her. If he did, she reasoned, then of course he would treat her with respect and caring. That seldom happened in their marriage, though. In fact, Clark's lack of appreciation was one reason they divorced. And yet Carlene clung to that wish, even as Clark actually became more disrespectful. Fortunately, once Carlene realized what was happening, she was better able to stop fantasizing. She could let go of the illusion that she could ever convince Clark to appreciate her.

And what about someone like Bart Ross, the guy who was absolutely furious at Judge Lefkow? What could he have wanted so desperately that he would kill because he didn't get it? Respect? Approval? Sympathy? Nurturing? We'll probably never know. But something deep inside him wouldn't let go. It drove him to seek first validation, then vindication.

Please think again about situations in which you have trouble letting go. Is there a pattern you can recognize? Can you identify what you want that you aren't getting? Which of your most important wants aren't getting met? Do you need to accept the reality that they aren't going to get met, at least not by that particular person or in the way you want? Do you need to let go of a fantasy in order to get back to reality?

STEP 4. *Challenge your fears about the terrible disasters you think will happen if you don't get what you want from someone.*

Carlene fears that Clark will turn their children against her. She dreads the day they will tell her they want to live only with their father. That's one big reason she tries to counter every single one of his lies, exaggerations, and manipulations. But no matter how hard she works at it, Clark always comes up with another scheme. Carlene has basically given all her power to Clark. It's as if he controlled her destiny. She wants her kids. She needs her kids. She can't live without them. And he can take them away. No wonder she's so worried and frustrated. Carlene's anger grows with each game he plays. So do her feelings of helplessness and weakness. That sets the stage for another impotent rage.

Carlene needs to challenge these terrible fears. How? First, she needs to gather accurate information. Her kids don't want to live all the time with their dad. They're smart enough not to get fooled by his tricks. Next, she needs to remind herself of her strengths. For example, she's smart enough to protect herself when she needs to. Yes, Clark is shifty and sneaky, but he is not going to take their children away from Carlene. Finally, at a more spiritual level, Carlene knows she can survive anything, even losing her children. Maybe Clark could take them from her, but even that would not defeat her.

People set themselves up for impotent rages when they fail to challenge their irrational fears.

Here are some questions for you: What disasters do you dread happening if you can't get what you want or need from someone else? What could you think or say that would help you let go of your fears? What power over your life have you given away to others?

STEP 5. *Reclaim your personal power with specific actions and thoughts.*

If impotent rages were plants, they would be the kind that grow best in poor dirt. They are best prevented by adding nutrients to the soil. And personal empowerment is the best nutrient on the market.

Carlene, for instance, needs to come up with a plan for what to do when her children are off with Clark. That's when she worries the most. She usually stays home and frets the whole time they're away. She stews. She gets angrier and angrier. She's ready for an impotent rage. Instead, she decides to get out of the house more. She begins by going for coffee with a friend. Two weeks later, she goes out for a movie and dinner. Eventually, she's ready for the big test: a weeklong vacation trip. She has to face down her fears, of course. That means reassuring herself that her children will still be hers when she gets back. But off she goes, feeling stronger and more self-confident than she has in years.

Each person's situation is unique, so what you need to do will be different from Carlene. The idea is to notice when you feel weak or when your life seems to be in someone else's hands. Then find ways to take back control of your life during those times. But don't try to control someone else. Keep the focus upon what you can do for yourself. That's how you can regain a sense of personal power.

Ask yourself these questions: When do you feel weakest, as if someone else had control of your life? What could you do to take better care of yourself during those times? How would doing those things help you feel stronger and more in control of your own fate?

STEP 6. *Consider forgiving those who have hurt you in order to let go of your simmering anger toward them.*

The more you think about something bad that happened to you, the worse you usually feel. The ultimate result is obsession, an inability to think about anything other than the insult or injury suffered. Obsession can easily turn into impotent rage as you replay these negative events. It's bad enough to feel helpless on one occasion. But if you can't let go of an old wound, helplessness, anger, and a desire for revenge can merge into a feeling of absolute hate toward the person who harmed you. How far away can an impotent rage be under those circumstances?

But how do you let go of that feeling of hate? Forgiving the person who harmed you is one answer. One definition of forgiving is "to let go of resentment and release the offender from possible retaliation" (Freedman 1999, 39). You need to free yourself from the idea that you can't let go of a bad memory until the person who harmed you has been punished.

Forgiving is a slow and difficult process. It is not for everyone or every situation. Many times it is simply easier to let go and walk away from a painful person than to work at forgiving him or her. But forgiving can help you quit simmering with anger over ancient wounds. That makes it a useful way to prevent the development of impotent rages.

Remember, the key to prevention is to gain a sense of personal control. One approach is to find a way to manage certain aspects of the bigger issue. Sometimes you also need to accept what you cannot change and move on to more rewarding things in life.

7

Shame-Based Rage

Harry: A Man Who Often Feels Disrespected

Harry is a thirty-year-old handyman and carpenter. Married to Susan, he has three young children. Although Harry wants to be happy with the blessings in his life, he has a big problem. Harry is super sensitive to criticism. Yesterday, for example, Harry was building a deck for a client when the man came out to ask how long Harry was going to be working. Harry took immediate offense. He was certain his client was implying that he was milking the job for extra hours. Harry got so mad that his face turned purple. He cursed the man and stomped off, leaving his expensive saws and tools behind. He came home to a phone call telling him he was fired and to a confused wife. "What happened?" she asked. That's when Harry blew another rod. "Don't you start in on me, too!" he screamed. Then he began yelling at the kids. "I tell you to pick up your toys, and you don't do it. You never listen to me! It says right in the Bible that children should obey their father, but you don't." Then Harry launched into his all-too-familiar life complaint: nobody respects him today, nobody ever respected him in the past, and as far as he's concerned, the whole world can go straight to hell. The more Harry ranted, the angrier he got. He scared his family. Fortunately, part of his brain stayed rational enough to tell Harry to leave the house. Off he went to spend another night in a motel room.

Harry admits he has a rage problem. He has gotten so angry at times that he's blacked out in anger. Here's what he says: "When people ignore me, disrespect me, or put me down, I get angry right away. Sometimes the anger feels like a time bomb ready to explode, and sometimes it leaves me feeling like the life has been sucked out of me."

Harry certainly has a rage problem. But this rage is different from the ones discussed earlier in the book. It's not about physical danger (survival rage). It doesn't happen because Harry feels powerless (impotent rage). Instead, Harry's shame is linked to his tremendous oversensitivity to criticism. Harry can't stand feeling insulted. He reacts to even the slightest criticism as if he had been smacked with a club. He becomes instantly outraged, defensive, and aggressive. Notice, also, that the issue isn't whether someone else actually intends to insult Harry. Harry often takes offense because he thinks someone is slighting him. Why, just the other day, Sue simply reminded him to pick up some diapers for the baby on his way home. His response: "I said I would do that this morning, didn't I? What do you think I am, an idiot? You never give me credit for anything." Harry went on for ten minutes about how disrespectful Sue was toward him. He got so mad, he drove right past the grocery store and came home empty-handed.

Shame-Based Rage

Harry has shame-based rages. Whenever Harry feels ashamed, he immediately becomes irate. He transfers his shame into anger because it's easier for him to feel mad than ashamed. Harry turns from feeling bad about himself to making others feel rotten. He exchanges shame for blame. He shames others, so he won't feel his own shame. Shame and blame is the name of his game.

Shame-based rages can be dangerous. They can even be fatal. Many murders have been committed by people who felt insulted. These attacks often take place at home against the very people the murderer loves most. But something happens, perhaps a wife saying something that shames her husband (or vice versa), and five minutes later someone is dead. Far more frequently, though, shame-based rages leave everybody feeling emotionally damaged and exhausted. The targets of shame-based rages often end up terribly confused as well. What happened here? Why did you say that awful, mean thing to me? Why did you feel so insulted when all I asked was a simple question? What can I say to you that doesn't feel like a criticism? And, maybe most painfully, what's wrong with you?

Well, something is wrong when moments of shame turn into rage. To see how that happens, though, it's important to understand the emotion of shame.

Shame

Shame is both a feeling and a belief. The feeling is very unpleasant. People usually talk about noticing their faces getting red, wanting to run away but finding themselves virtually paralyzed, being unable to maintain eye contact with anyone, losing all their strength and becoming incredibly weak and powerless, feeling totally exposed to people's scrutiny and criticism, and collapsing inside into nothingness. This feeling can be almost unendurable. That's why people find ways to make it go away, including converting shame into rage.

The belief that goes with shame is that somehow you are defective. Broken. Useless. Flawed. Damaged goods. Ugly. Worthless. The deeper the shame, the more this damage seems impossible to mend. Eventually, powerfully shamed people come to believe these messages:

- "I am no good."

- "I am not good enough."

- "I am unlovable."

- "I don't belong."

- "I should not exist."

These are terribly damaging messages. People who think this way about themselves suffer. They see themselves as total losers.

Shame affects people's behavior as well. Strongly shamed people tend to avoid others. That's because they are sure everyone else will see all their flaws. They might not want to talk about themselves either, for the same reason. As with Harry, they may also be very touchy, making them unpredictable and difficult to live with.

Shame also has a spiritual component. Deeply shamed individuals often feel cut off from spiritual support. Judging themselves as unworthy of love or respect, they think of themselves as God's mistake. Consequently, they often feel empty inside.

Shame Makes You Want to Hide

The instinctive way to react to a moment of shame is to want to hide or run away. The goal is to become invisible, so nobody can see your defects. This natural desire to withdraw helps shamed people feel safer. However, leaving the scene when feeling ashamed comes with a price—you take your feelings of weakness and brokenness with you. Also, the research on shame shows that deeply shamed people are poor communicators. Relationship problems don't get resolved by running away. True, strong shame is an awful feeling. But you cannot learn to deal with shame when all you do is flee from it. Even sadder is that running away from shame triggers a self-defeating spiral. The more you flee your shame, the worse you feel about yourself (because fleeing anything is itself a sign of shameful weakness). The worse you feel about yourself, the more you flee from anything that might produce more shame. That makes you feel ever more sensitive to shame, so that smaller and smaller incidents unleash stronger and stronger feelings of shame. Eventually tiny incidents trigger mountains of shame.

That's what happened to Harry. He's become so oversensitized to shame that he completely misinterpreted his customer's innocent question: "Harry, how long will you be working today?" Harry heard,

"Harry, I'm on to your game. You're trying to stretch the clock. You're pathetic. Shame on you." He acted on his shame when he ran away. But first he attacked, cursing his customer. Why?

From Shame to Rage

Shame always feels rotten. It's bad enough when you are prepared for it. At least then, you can do a little internal damage control. But Harry wasn't prepared at all. He was just finishing his day when along came what felt to him like a sudden, unprovoked attack. Harry felt instantaneous shame. Intolerable shame. Defectiveness at the core of his being. That shame was simply too much for him to bear. He had to get away from his shame as quickly as possible.

There is one magical way to get rid of something you don't want. Give it to someone else. Play "I don't want it, you can have it." And that's what Harry did before he left the scene. Like someone returning an unwanted Christmas present to its giver, Harry tried to return the shame to the shamer. Harry had to get rid of at least some of his shame before he left, and he did so by trying to humiliate the other guy. His shame was just too painful to keep. Feeling attacked, Harry became the aggressor.

Harry's reaction would only be a shame-anger response if this were all there was to it. But there's more. In fact, there's magic in the shame-rage response—mental and emotional magic, that is. Sleight of mind instead of sleight of hand. Just ask Harry what he felt when his customer wanted to know how long he'd be working. He'd say, "Man, I was really pissed off. That's what I felt. Really, really mad." Do you notice what's missing? Harry's not saying anything about shame. That's because he converted his shame into rage so quickly that he didn't even consciously notice his shame. His body certainly felt shame. That's why he reacted so strongly. But all Harry noticed was his immediate anger. Harry has pushed his shameful feelings out of conscious awareness. He has replaced them with rage.

Harry does everything he can to escape his shame. All the way home, he thinks about what a jerk that customer was and how he had every right to tell him off. He would never use the word "shame" to describe how he feels. But he feels crappy, exhausted, vulnerable. No wonder he takes offense at the first words out of his wife's mouth. More shame! So now he goes after her, and then the kids. Harry is haunted by a terrible feeling he cannot allow himself to name. He is full of shame.

The shame-rage message is scary: "You are shaming me. What you are saying makes me feel weak and powerless. I am humiliated. It feels like you are trying to destroy me. I can't let that happen. Instead, I must attack you. I have to shame you. I need to force you to take my shame before it kills me. I have to make you feel even weaker than me. I might even have to destroy you."

How Vulnerable Are You to Shame-Based Rage?

Shame-based rage is terrifying and dangerous. If you have shame-rage episodes, you need to recognize them. Otherwise, you won't be able to stop them. So ask yourself these questions:

- Do people say that you are way too sensitive to criticism?

- Do people often tell you that they don't understand why something they said bothered you so much?

- Do you become furious when people seem to disrespect you?

- Is your reputation—your good name—something you strongly defend?

- Do you frequently worry that people think you are stupid, worthless, ugly, or incompetent?

- Do you get really mad after a moment of embarrassment, for instance, if someone points out something you did wrong?

- Do you dwell upon put-downs that you believe people have made about you?

- Do you become irate when people seem to be ignoring you?

- Is anger, even really strong anger, easier for you to handle than feeling shame?

- Do you sense that you convert feelings of shame to anger or rage?

The more you answered yes to the questions above, the more likely you are to have problems with shame rage. The rest of this chapter describes ways to prevent and contain shame-based rages.

Taming Shame-Based Rage

If you experience shame-based rage, you know you're living with an untamed beast inside your head. That creature is dangerous, especially if it sneaks up on you. It's powerful enough to kill. It's unpredictable, too, so you never quite know what will set it off. You really can't afford to let the shame-rage monster keep stalking its prey. You've got to find a way to cage that rage and then tame it, so you can get back in control of your life.

Fortunately, there are nine steps you can take to tame shame-based rage.

STEP 1. *Make a strong commitment right now to gain control over shame-based rage.*

Harry's had it. As they say in Alcoholics Anonymous, he's sick and tired of feeling sick and tired. Mostly, he's beginning to hate himself because of his rages. "I keep shooting myself in the foot," he says. He's right, too. His rages are destroying everything important to him: his marriage, his relationships with his children, his career. Like many ragers, Harry has clung to the illusion that he cannot control these bouts of extreme anger. Up until now, all he's done is apologize after the fact. But "I'm so sorry, I don't know why I yelled at you. I didn't mean it when I called you that" gets old after a while. Besides, Harry can't heal his shame when he keeps doing things that only make him feel even worse about himself.

Harry's ready to make a strong commitment to change. First, he must quit giving himself any wiggle room. That means accepting no excuses for raging. No "I was having a bad day" or "It was the way she said it that really pissed me off." No "I couldn't help it" or "I know I shouldn't have done that, but…" And, most importantly, no "I'll try to quit raging." Trying won't work. Harry must commit to stopping his shame-based rages in their tracks each and every time.

Now, of course it takes more than just a promise to yourself to quit raging. That's why I've described several additional steps below. However, a strong commitment not to rage is absolutely essential when confronting shame-based rages.

So what happens if Harry cannot keep this pledge? What if he has another rage? Then he must do everything in his power to figure out what happened. He must make amends to the people he hurt. And he must keep working on changing what he thinks, says, and does until he frees himself from his raging.

Here's a place to make your own promise to break free from shame-based rages. Write your name in the blank space.

I, _____, promise today to quit raging. Specifically, I will refrain from raging against anybody, especially the people I love. If I feel personally shamed by something others say or do, I will step away until I gain control over my urge to attack. I will use no excuses to justify shaming, blaming, or treating others with contempt.

How important is this to you? Do you need to make this promise today?

STEP 2. *Follow the shame-rage trail back to your own shameful thoughts and feelings.*

Shame-based rages almost always feel like they are triggered by something another person says or does. But it's actually more complicated than that. The real trigger for a shame-rage episode is what goes on inside your head. So, if you want to learn all you can about your raging, you will need to learn more about your own thoughts and feelings. To do so, you'll be like an explorer, temporarily lost, who finds the way back to camp by following the trail you left behind.

Imagine standing outside yourself, watching, as you begin having a shame-based rage. What would you see? What if you could hear your thoughts right then, as if they were coming from someone else? What would you hear? You'll need to become a good observer of yourself if you want to end shame-based raging. Most importantly, you'll need to learn exactly what happens inside your brain right before you rage.

It can be painful to look inside yourself, especially if you feel a lot of shame. Who of us wants to notice times when we are feeling bad about ourselves? It's tempting to focus upon the other person instead, blaming them for making you feel bad. But it's not them you need to be concerned about. It's you.

It's easier to begin, though, from the outside, at the end of the shame-rage trail. Here you can review what triggers your shame-based rage. If you are prone to shame-based rages, you probably have a set of things people might say or imply that would really bother you. Here are several examples: "She says I'm self-centered." "He thinks I'm stupid." "He calls me lazy." "They completely ignore me." "She treats me like a fool." Please notice that these statements are all very generalized. They aren't about specific behavior. Instead, they label you. They say bad things about your personality, things that would be hard to change if true. They attack the center of your being. These labels suggest that there is something wrong about you, that you are deeply flawed. They are shaming. That's why they hurt so much.

Sometimes people really say or do these things. They may even be deliberately trying to shame you. You will need to challenge these people and insist upon respectful treatment. However, the mere fact that someone calls you a name is never enough to trigger a shame-rage explosion. There must also be a voice inside of you that at least partly agrees with your accusers. That voice, your own voice, says, "You know, she's right. I am an idiot." That voice is your shame. It reminds you constantly of everything inadequate about you.

Here's proof that what triggers a shame-rage episode is what goes on inside you, not outside. Just imagine someone shaming you, perhaps by calling you one of those names above. As you imagine this, you probably will begin to have shameful feelings, as well as angry feelings toward the other person. But nobody is actually insulting you. Again, it's what goes on in your head that's critical. Besides, you can feel shame even when no attack is intended. Harry, for example, believed that his client was deliberately putting him down. But he was wrong. His real attacker was his own shame. That shame led Harry to mistakenly interpret his customer's question as an attack.

When you follow the shame-rage trail, it leads back from what others say and do to your own shaming thoughts. These thoughts might take many forms, such as "I am damaged goods," "I am pitiful," "I am worthless," "I am dirty," "I am weak," "I am unwanted," or "I am nothing at all." But don't stop there. Keep moving on, and you'll eventually reach the five core shame statements: "I am no good." "I am not good enough." "I am unlovable." "I don't belong." "I should not exist."

This is the end of the trail. Here is where all shame-rage episodes begin.

STEP 3. *Discover how you temporarily get rid of your shame by raging.*

The scene at the trailhead inside your brain isn't peaceful. Instead, there's a huge argument going on. One part of you is shouting out that you are useless, worthless, fat, a stupid ignoramus, that you are not good enough, that you are God's mistake. That's your shame. The other part of you is covering its ears, stomping its feet, and screaming, "I am not useless, I am not stupid, I am not fat, I'm not an ignoramus. I am too good enough. I'm not a mistake." That's your rage. It desperately wants to make your shame go away. Finally, your rage reaches over and grabs that shame. It twirls it around and around like a professional wrestling champion. And then it throws that shame right out of the ring, completely out of your mind.

Do you know where that shame lands? Right in somebody else's lap. "Aha," your brain says. "I knew it all along. It's not me who's shameful. It's him. It's her. It's them." Now you can call these people all the terrible things your shame was saying about you. They're the ones who are ugly, dumb, worthless, and bad. You attack them without even realizing that you're still really attacking yourself. It works for a while, too. You feel strong, powerful, in control. The other people are the ones who are weak and helpless, not you.

There's a catch, though. Your shame is clever. It has a way of sneaking back into your campsite. It can show up at the trailhead just about any time. Then you'll have that same battle, usually with the same result. It's exhausting. Meanwhile, like Harry, you might get fired from your job and face losing your family.

STEP 4. *Reclaim your shame to break the shame-rage connection.*

There is only one way to stop this. It isn't easy. You'll have to listen to the self-attacking part of your own personality, to the part of you that says you are shameful. But there's simply no alternative. Either confront your own inner shame or continue to risk having more shame-rage episodes. Now nobody says you should go up and hug that shame like a long-lost brother. You don't have to embrace something that feels so bad. Just accept it. Listen to the messages. After all, that inner shame has been part of your life for a long time. The only difference is that now you are ready to pay attention to it.

You can and will survive facing your shame head-on. It won't destroy you. Why do I emphasize this? Because deep shame is intimidating. It may seem too powerful to endure. That's where the real power of shame lies. People convert their shame to rage when they secretly doubt they can live through their awful shameful feelings. In one sense, then, it is not the shame itself but your fear of the shame that triggers shame rage. Once you know that you can survive your shame, you can handle it better. Most critically, you can keep your shame under conscious control.

Practically speaking, this means you should always ask yourself one question whenever you start getting really angry: "Hey—wait a minute—is this about my shame?" Then take some time to think about it. Carefully, slowly, trace the shame back to the five core shaming messages mentioned above. But also remember one more important idea: just because a part of you calls you shameful doesn't make it true.

STEP 5. *Challenge the validity of the five core shame messages.*

So far, you have carefully examined how your shameful feelings get turned into rage. All that is useful, but here is the most important thing to do to stop shame-based raging. You must consciously confront your shame. It's time to challenge those negative, shaming thoughts you have. It's necessary to replace them with healing thoughts. Each core shame message must ultimately be replaced by a healthier message that doesn't trigger shame-rage episodes. You can do that best by focusing upon the five core shaming messages and changing each of them into its opposite. Imagine going from

- "I am no good" to "I am good."

- "I am not good enough" to "I am good enough."

- "I am unlovable" to "I am loved and lovable."

- "I don't belong" to "I belong."

- "I should not exist" to "I am."

It might be a good idea right now to say these five positive phrases out loud, slowly, repeating them several times. Which of these positive phrases feel very true to you? Which feel a little true? Do any feel completely false? Those phrases that feel least accurate are the ones you'll have to focus on the longest so that you can accept them.

The next step is for you to think of other, related thoughts that you need to change. For example, you might need to alter "I am ugly" to "I am beautiful." If "I am beautiful" is asking too much for now, how about "I look okay" or "I am fairly attractive" or "I am who I am"? You'll need to try on a lot of healing phrases until you come up with several that feel helpful and healing to you. Then keep saying them to yourself, every day, so your brain can get into the habit of positive self-regard.

Challenging your shameful thoughts can be frustrating. Nobody I know has ever immediately gone from "I'm no good" to "I'm good." Some days you may feel really good about yourself, and other days you may be full of self-hatred. This is a process that only takes a moment to begin but may take a lifetime to complete. Please be kind to yourself as you walk this new trail toward self-worth and self-acceptance.

So how do you do it? Patiently. Calmly. Optimistically. Fortunately, you can expect to feel a little better about yourself just because you are moving along this path. Walking the trail itself is healing.

Here are some questions that could help you become less self-shaming and more self-approving:

- What thoughts do you already have that help you believe in your own essential goodness?

- What new thoughts could you think that would also help in this way?

- What do you do that helps you feel you are making a contribution to the world?

- Who in your life regularly respects you, praises you, and/or appreciates you?

- How are you kind to and accepting and forgiving of yourself?

- How else could you become kinder to and more accepting and forgiving of yourself?

STEP 6. *Treat others with respect and dignity at all times.*

It is too easy, if you are someone with shame-based rage, to concentrate only upon how people are treating you. "Does he respect me? Is she putting me down? Are they ignoring me?" You can become paranoid this way, constantly looking for the tiniest signs that others disrespect you. There's something better you could do with your time, though. You could focus upon treating others with respect. Basically, then, you'd be giving others the gift you most appreciate receiving. That act of generosity would ultimately benefit you a lot, as well. First, you will think less about your worries and self-doubts. Second, it's likely that people you treat decently will return the favor. If you don't shame them, they will be less likely to shame you. And, third, you will probably feel good about yourself when you act like a gentleman or a lady. That will help you heal the shame that triggers rages.

Now let's get more specific. Here are some ideas on how to treat others with respect:

Begin your day with a strong commitment that you will treat everybody respectfully, no matter what they say and do. This puts you, not them, in charge of your actions.

Look for the inner goodness of each person in your life. Respect for others is based upon appreciating them as human beings. Take time to notice how each person is unique, worthy, and admirable. In doing so, you are responding to their need to feel "I am" with a strong "Yes, you are, and that is good." You are helping celebrate their existence.

Be sure to tell others, especially the people closest to you, that they are good, good enough, and loved. Help them feel that they have a place (in your family, in the universe, in your heart). Don't let those words get stuck in your throat. They do a lot more good when said aloud than when you only think them to yourself.

Use the five As as aids to treating others respectfully (Potter-Efron 2001). The letter A happens to be very useful in thinking about respect. At least five words that begin with A offer ways to be respectful:

Attend: "I'll take time to really listen to you. I will give you my complete attention."

Appreciate: "I like what you do. I like how you do things."

Accept: "You don't have to change. You are okay the way you are."

Admire: "I can learn from you. You do things with grace and skill."

Affirm: "I am happy that you are part of my life. I want to celebrate your existence."

Remembering these five words will help you become more respectful of others. You can use them as a mental checklist: "Have I paid good attention to people today? Have I shown appreciation? Have I been accepting? Have I let myself learn from anyone today? Have I been affirming?"

STEP 7. *Give praise instead of criticism.*

What did Harry do when he was in the middle of his shame-rage episode? He became extremely critical of his client, wife, and children. That's typical. Criticism is the main tool in the shamer's toolbox. Indeed, being critical of others becomes a self-fulfilling habit. You can always find something wrong with people when you go looking for it. The trouble is that being so negative toward others only sets you up for another rage. When all you see is what's bad in others, then you start believing they are going to do bad things to you. Fortunately, there is a way to break the habit of criticism. You must learn to give praise instead of criticism, to look for the good instead of the bad in others. Praise is in many ways the exact opposite of shame. While shaming and criticizing make people feel small and weak, giving praise makes them feel tall and strong.

Praising others is more than an act of generosity or a way to be nice if you have shame-based rages. It is a way to prevent those rages from developing. Remember that shame-ragers are trying to give their own shame to others. Constantly criticizing others is only a diversion from the real work you need to do, namely finding ways to better accept and appreciate yourself. The shame-rager's message looks like this: "You are bad and I am good." But it's really this: "I'm bad, but I don't want to admit it."

There are many ways to praise people. First, notice their accomplishments, effort, thoughtfulness, creativity, generosity, appearance, individuality, and intelligence. Then tell them about it. Just be sure never to follow praise with the word "but," as "your hair looks nice, but..." Don't use praise as an opening to criticism if you want the praise to be believed.

Get into the habit of praising others. That will help you with the even harder work of learning to appreciate yourself. Ultimately, that's the only way to break free from shame-based rage.

STEP 8. *Surround yourself with people who treat you respectfully.*

Many, perhaps most, people with shame-based rage grew up painfully. Their families may have been afflicted with alcoholism, grinding poverty, mental illness, or disease. As children, they may have been the target of physical or sexual abuse. They may have been scapegoated, or blamed for the family's troubles. Their parents may have been critical, hostile, or neglectful. In other words, they may have grown up in families where shaming and blaming were the norm.

That's why it's important to surround yourself with people who treat you with respect. Shame-ragers simply cannot afford to hang around too many negative people. It's just not healthy. Worse, you are far more likely to rage under these circumstances. It's much easier, after all, to rage at someone who really has just put you down than at someone who is being respectful.

You always have to work on yourself first if you are a shame-rager. Don't go telling everybody else to get their act together when that's what you should be doing yourself. However, it is fair to expect others to treat you decently. In fact, it's really important. Nobody thrives in a shaming environment. And, frankly, it's much harder to stop shame-rage episodes when shaming and blaming envelop a family like a dense fog. So here is the natural sequence of events: do everything you can to heal your shame; treat others with respect at all times; ask, expect, and, if necessary, insist that others treat you with respect; seriously consider leaving situations in which people continue to be shaming, critical, hostile, or neglectful; gather as many positive, caring, respectful people as you can into your world. Become a collector of people with goodwill. But remember that you must be a model of that goodwill, as well.

STEP 9. Watch for relapse signs that your shame rage is getting out of control.

The goal of all these steps is to prevent shame-rage episodes. You will need to take time to go through them. Above all, you will need to make a long-term effort to improve your own personal sense of self-worth. You must journey from shameful self-hatred to a positive sense of yourself as good and good enough. That may be a long journey. But every step you take on the path toward self-acceptance and self-love lessens the risk of raging. Meanwhile, though, you will need to stay on guard for any hints that you are heading in the wrong direction, back toward rage. One way to do this is to make a list of shame-rage predictors. These are things you have thought, ways you have felt, and stuff you have done a few minutes or hours before you raged. A typical list might look like this:

Rage-predicting thoughts: "She doesn't appreciate me." "I'm worthless." "He thinks he's better than me." "I hate myself." "What's the use?" "They're stupid." "Who do they think they are?"

Rage-predicting feelings: "I'm really tense." "I'm getting mad." "I feel weird." "I can feel a rage coming." "I'm losing control."

Rage-predicting actions: "I'm starting to get mean." "I'm pacing again." "I'm getting loud."

Some shame-rage predictors occur well in advance, maybe even days before an episode. These tend to be rather vague and generalized, such as "I just don't feel quite right" or "Uh-oh." Trouble's on the way." Maybe you'll feel a little down, somewhat depressed. But it's probably not really depression. What's happening is that shame has snuck back into your brain. It's making you feel weak and sad. Pretty soon, if you just let this go on, you'll feel so bad about yourself that you will need to get rid of the shame through raging. However, raging is not inevitable. It is never inevitable. But you will need to take the time and make the effort to deal with those bad feelings you're having about yourself. It's important to challenge that shame whenever it threatens to take over your life.

Other cues that you're heading for a rage might only happen a minute or two before the blow: a sudden flash of anger; a nasty thought that seems to come from nowhere; the feeling that you are being put down. These last-minute cues are like looking up while you're taking a walk and seeing a monstrous storm heading toward you. You'll just have time, if you hurry, to get to shelter. The first thing to do is to try to calm down. Take a few deep breaths. Remind yourself not to start attacking. Don't let yourself begin raging. But if you are really close to losing control, you'll need to take a time-out and get away from people immediately.

Whatever happens, never give up on yourself. Never believe that you cannot control shame-based rages. Keep working to feel better about yourself and the world. In the long run that's the only way to quit raging.

Abandonment Rage

8

Bettina: A Woman Who Fears Abandonment

Bettina is a forty-year-old personnel manager at a major local factory.

"Quit whining. I put the gun down, didn't I?" Those are the first words she says to her partner of two years, Mason, as he tries to explain why they are going to marriage counseling. "Yeah," Mason replies, "but you really scared me. You went crazy. I thought you were going to pull the trigger." "Well," she answers, "You said you might leave me." To Bettina, apparently, that possibility is enough to justify any action she might take, up to and including murder.

As you might expect, this episode isn't the first time Bettina has blown sky high in her relationship with Mason. She has repeatedly pulled his hair, locked him out of the house, locked him in the house, slapped his face, and spat on him. Bettina is also extremely jealous, threatening to maim him if he even so much as glances at another woman. She accuses many women of trying to lure Mason away, but then she always shifts the focus onto him, blaming him for flirting with every skirt in sight. The fact that Mason has actually been totally loyal to Bettina, never coming close to cheating on her, seems not to have penetrated her brain. She's convinced that, sooner or later, he's going to mess around "because that's what men do."

Bettina's had the same problem in every significant relationship she's ever had. Indeed, she admits that she's driven men away with a combination of tremendous neediness, irrational jealousy, and desperate insecurity. Bettina recognizes that she's essentially created her own personal misery, and yet she can't seem to stop. "I hate myself for being this way. I know I scare men off. But I can't stand being alone. I feel so empty inside. When Mason says he needs a little time apart from me, I feel like I'm gonna die. I get scared. Then I get mad. I remember the times I've been left alone and the times I've been cheated on, and I become absolutely furious. That's when I go nuts. It's like I want to make him pay for all those times in the past when I was abandoned."

How far back does Bettina's history of abandonment go? All the way to childhood. The last memory she has of her father is of him packing his bags and leaving home without a word, never to return, when Bettina was seven years old. But her father was never really a part of her life. He'd be home a few days or weeks, then leave, and then return unpredictably throughout her early childhood. Sometimes he'd promise that things would be different, that he would stick around for his little girl, but he never did. Bettina quit trusting his word after several of these false promises.

Bettina's mother wasn't a whole lot more dependable, either. She became addicted to alcohol and to alcoholics, especially after Bettina's father moved out for good. Sometimes that meant Bettina was left alone all night, feeling unsafe. But that was better than when Mom would show up at three in the morning with a drunken sot of a boyfriend. Bettina locked herself in her bedroom on those occasions, not because she was afraid of assault but because she dreaded hearing yet another one promising to take care of her and her mom, only to leave within hours or days.

Bettina has a definite rage pattern. But notice the differences between her rages and the kinds discussed in previous chapters. Bettina's not concerned about being in physical danger (survival rage). Although she certainly doesn't feel in control, she doesn't feel powerless to affect her situation (impotent rage). Nor is shame the source of her raging. The true cause of Bettina's rage is her fear, actually her terror, of abandonment.

Abandonment rage is a feeling of tremendous fury that is triggered by real or imagined threats of abandonment, betrayal, or neglect.

Abandonment Rage Begins in Childhood

John Bowlby, a brilliant researcher who lived in England in the twentieth century, is the father of what has become known as *attachment theory* (Bowlby 1969, 1973, 1980). He discovered that young children make powerful and long-lasting decisions about how reliable the world is and will be. Although they can't say so in words, basically children ask themselves questions like these:

- "Can I count on my caregivers to be there for me when I need them?"

- "Will people who say they care treat me well or poorly?"

- "How much can I trust my caregivers to keep their promises?"

- "How safe or dangerous are my caregivers? Do they protect me from danger, or are they themselves dangerous to me?"

- "How consistent or inconsistent are my caregivers?"

- "Will my caregivers stick around, or will they abandon me?"

- "Do my caregivers love me completely and unconditionally, or do they quit loving me if I say or do something they don't like?"

- "How safe or unsafe are people? How safe or unsafe is the world?"

These questions can be boiled down to one big question: "How much can I depend on the people who should love me and take care of me?"

Amazingly, children pretty much decide the answers to these questions by eighteen months of age. They form what is called an *internal working model* of reality (Bowlby 1969, 1973, 1980). That model acts like a cookie cutter or a template in their heads. From then on, they expect anyone who should be caring and loving with them to act in the ways predicted by the model. Bettina, for instance, decided long ago that nobody could be trusted, least of all men who say she can depend upon them. She's sure at a deep level that any such man, like her father, will make promises he won't keep and eventually abandon her. Indeed, she's so convinced of this inevitability that nothing nice Mason does gets through to her. Mason's loyalty means nothing, since, after all, no matter how trustworthy he seems, he could cheat on her or leave her down the road. In Bettina's eyes, she's made yet another emotional investment in someone who won't make one back. No wonder she's scared and angry.

Before continuing, you might want to take a good look at the set of questions above. Take a few minutes to answer them carefully. Don't just think about them, either. Instead, notice how you feel in response to each query. Pay particular attention to that last question: "How much can I depend on the people who should love me and take care of me?" Your answer to that question says a lot about how likely you are to have abandonment rages.

Kids Don't Let Go of Their Caregivers Without a Fight

I remember a time my wife Pat and I tried to go to the movies when our first child, Cindy, was about a year old. She didn't like that idea one bit. First she held out her arms to us. When that didn't work, she turned red. She cried. She screamed. She fought. She would not be consoled. And she wouldn't quit. Finally, the babysitter told us just to go. We left, feeling guilty. She finally did quit crying, the babysitter said, but not for another fifteen minutes.

To understand what that's all about, you have to place yourself in a child's mind. To Cindy and to all children of that age, there is no such thing as a temporary departure. How can they know that Mommy and Daddy will be back in just a few hours when they do not yet understand what that means? Besides, infants and young children cannot survive without adult caregivers. They need adults in their lives to live. So, in the face of loss, they protest. But to say that children "protest" the loss of their caregivers is a severe understatement. What they do is rage. If they could put words right then to their emotion, they would say something like this: "How dare you leave me! You don't care if I live or die, do you? I hate you. I hate you. I hate you. But please, please come back, because I need you so bad."

Right there is the foundation for adult abandonment rages. Adults like Bettina are saying and feeling the same things as those children. They too are protesting against the loss of a desperately needed person. They also feel that combination of absolute hate and desperate neediness.

Still, not all children grow up to be adults who fly into rages at the mere thought of someone leaving them. It's children like Bettina, who grow up in unstable environments, who most frequently become abandonment ragers.

Feeling Secure vs. Feeling Insecure in Relationships

"It is easy for me to become emotionally close to others. I am comfortable depending upon others and having others depend upon me. I don't worry about being alone or having others not accept me" (Feeney, Noller, and Hanrahan 1994, 131).

How much do you agree with the statement above? These are typical thoughts of people who feel quite confident and comfortable in their relationships. People who strongly agree with this statement are often called *secure* by researchers who study how people attach to each other (Feeney, Noller, and Hanrahan 1994).

If you were fortunate enough to be raised with at least one healthy, consistent, and loving parent (or stepparent, grandparent, or someone else who could provide stability), then you probably feel fairly secure in your relationships. By that, I mean you expect the people you love to stick around. You figure they will keep their promises. You basically trust people. In addition, chances are you don't get too anxious when your partner goes away for a few hours or even longer. You fully expect him or her to return to you. You are confident that your partner wants you in his or her life. Sure, you may have moments of jealousy and insecurity. But a little reassurance ("Honey, don't worry. I'll be home as soon as I can. I love you") will usually be all it takes for you to feel safe again. All these good feelings mean that you don't need to protest loudly every time your partner separates from you. You won't rage.

Here is another quote. "I want to be completely emotionally intimate with others, but I often find that others are reluctant to get as close as I would like. I am uncomfortable being without close relationships, but I sometimes worry that others don't value me as much as I value them" (Feeney, Noller, and Hanrahan 1994, 131). These words describe people who easily become *preoccupied* in their relationships (Feeney, Noller, and Hanrahan 1994). They continually worry about being abandoned by the people they love and need. Highly anxious, they feel compelled to stay in contact with their relationship partners. "Don't leave me" becomes a central theme between them and their partners. They often appear needy. But it's a demanding type of neediness, sometimes whiny ("Please, please, don't go. I can't live without you") and sometimes demanding ("You can't leave me. That's intolerable. I insist you stay"). The partners of these people sometimes feel smothered because of their partner's continual need to spend time together. How familiar are these thoughts to you? Would you say that you frequently fit this picture? How preoccupied do you become in your relationships?

Okay. How about this quote? "I am uncomfortable getting close to others. I want emotionally close relationships, but I find it difficult to trust others completely, or to depend on them. I worry that I will be hurt if I allow myself to become too close to others" (Feeney, Noller, and Hanrahan 1994, 131). These are the words of *fearful* individuals (Feeney, Noller, and Hanrahan 1994). What they fear most is rejection. Although these fearful individuals tend to avoid getting too involved at first, eventually they do jump in. However, their partners often find them to be vulnerable and emotionally fragile. That's because they remain convinced that their partners will eventually dump them. They just don't see themselves as "keepers." So they live every day on the edge of a cliff called abandonment, expecting their partner to push them off. Above all, these fearful people are distrusting. It is just plain difficult for them to believe that anyone would choose to stay loyal to them. This lack of trust eats away at their relationships, making it virtually impossible for them to feel really safe and secure. If you are fearful like this, you too are living scared, perhaps way too scared.

Which Attachment Pattern Best Fits You?

Real people are usually too complicated to fit neatly into any one attachment pattern. That means you might identify with feeling secure, preoccupied, or fearful on different occasions with the same person. Another possibility is that you may have felt secure in one relationship but are preoccupied or fearful in another. But the key question here is how often do you find yourself feeling preoccupied or fearful in your serious relationships, especially now?

So what do you think? Which of these patterns do you most identify with? Which one do you identify with second? Third? Would your partner agree with your rankings? Maybe you should ask him or her. Sometimes people think they are secure when their partners would call them preoccupied or fearful.

Perhaps you just aren't sure which attachment pattern fits best. Here's one way to find out. Ask yourself what you do when you face a temporary separation from your partner. Say when your partner says something like this: "Dear, I want to have one night out a week without you."

Do you protest? ("No, that's not okay. Why do you need time away from me anyhow? Does that mean you don't love me? Do you have someone else? Are you planning to leave me?") Do you become accusatory? ("I knew it. You're just like all the rest. I can't trust you at all, can I?") Do you become so wrapped up in your misery that you can't accept any explanation your partner gives, no matter how reasonable? (Your partner: "Honey, you get two nights off every week. I just want one evening to get away from the kids for a while. It doesn't mean I don't love you.") And then do you lose control? ("I hate you! You won't get away with this. I'm gonna make you pay.") Finally, do you soar into a full-fledged abandonment rage?

Here are some things that are true of preoccupied and fearful people who frequently have abandonment rages. How many apply to you?

- You become furious when you think about times when you have been abandoned or betrayed.

- You struggle with intense feelings of jealousy.

- You look for proof that people who say they care about you cannot be trusted.

- Feeling neglected or ignored by the people you love seems almost intolerable to you.

- You become preoccupied with wanting to get back at your parents or partners because they left you, neglected you, or betrayed you.

- You feel cheated by your partner, children, or friends because you give them way more love, care, and attention than you get back.

- You have been told that once you become really mad, you can't take in any reassurances or statements of caring from the people you are angry with.

If you are often preoccupied or fearful, then you probably feel insecure much of the time. This sense of insecurity, in turn, makes you vulnerable to having abandonment rages. That's because you cannot believe deep within your soul that your partner really wants you. Your uncertainty makes you continually question his or her loyalty. You are constantly on the alert, ready to protest loudly anything that hints at your partner leaving you. Your rage bubbles up from a core complaint: "Why won't anyone love me, hold me, comfort me, and make me feel safe?"

If you are vulnerable to abandonment rages, the rest of this chapter will help you learn how to prevent them. But first, consider what might have caused you to become preoccupied or fearful. Perhaps you were raised like Bettina, with nobody you could count on to be there when you needed them. Your parents may have been unavailable, unreliable, or unpredictable, for a number of reasons: illness or disease; alcoholism or addiction; disinterest or neglect; physical separation through war or work demands; emotional problems like incapacitating depression; mental illnesses such as schizophrenia; or marital separation or divorce, especially the messy kind where one parent tries to keep the children from seeing the other parent. Poverty also might have made it difficult for your parents to meet your needs. If these problems began early and lasted a long time, you may have greater insecurity than other people who had more stable upbringings. You would then be more likely to struggle with a nagging, scary sense that the people you love often think about leaving you, actually want to leave you, and most certainly will leave you.

Childhood isn't the only way people become insecure, though. Unhealthy adult relationships can strongly affect you. Certainly trying to love someone who really does lie, cheat, and steal is a formula for insecurity. Your entire relationship history, not just your family of origin, molds how you feel about relationship bonds.

How Can an Insecure Person Become More Secure?

When I use the terms "secure," "preoccupied," and "fearful" here, I am describing those deeply felt ideas about the world that John Bowlby called "internal working models." (There is a fourth attachment pattern, named *dismissive* [Feeney, Noller, and Hanrahan 1994]. Dismissers don't commit much to relationships. True dismissers are unlikely to have abandonment rages, which is why I only mention them briefly here.) Internal working models are the ideas about relationships that were formed by your eighteenth month of life. They are strong and deeply rooted. That means preoccupied and fearful people don't suddenly feel secure just because a relationship has gone well for a few days, or months, or even years. For that matter, secure people don't suddenly become insecure just because they've had a couple of bad days with their partner.

Fortunately, though, there is some good news here. A great deal of research has shown that people can and do change their attachment patterns over time. That means that no matter how insecure you feel today, there is reason to hope that you can learn how to feel better about yourself and safer within your relationships over time. True, you will have to be patient with yourself. But be hopeful. You can gain a real sense of security. Given the right conditions, your internal working model of reality can change. It usually does so gradually, though.

However, I do want to make one disclaimer here: no matter how much you want to feel safe, you can't move from feeling insecure to feeling secure if your real-life experiences continue to be with unsafe people. You will need to hang around trustworthy people in order to trust.

The stakes are high here. Changing your inner sense of relationship security is necessary if you struggle with abandonment rage. The long-term formula for quitting these rages is to feel more secure about yourself and the people you love.

How to Prevent Abandonment Raging

Here are the seven steps you must take to prevent abandonment rages.

STEP 1. *Learn everything you can about with whom, when, how, and why you turn your fear of rejection and abandonment into rage.*

There is a definite similarity between shame-based rage and abandonment rage. In both situations, the only visible emotion is extreme anger, but hiding underneath is another equally intense emotion. With shame-based rage, the feeling is shame. Abandonment rage covers a deep sense of fear, namely the fear of being abandoned. You will need to work backwards from the scene of the crime (your explosion) to discover how your rage masks other emotions. You must answer at least four questions in your detective work.

With whom do you rage? Abandonment rages typically are reserved for the people we love and need most in our lives. They are the people we believe we cannot live without—or that we believe life wouldn't be worth living without. The most likely candidates, then, are partners, ex-partners, parents, siblings, children, best friends, and important coworkers. Still, you might only rage at men or only at women. You might rage mostly at people who remind you of your parents. Perhaps you primarily rage at younger people or older ones. Take a good look at your raging pattern to see with whom you need to guard the most against raging. Remember that the best predictor of your next rage is the past, so the most likely targets for your next rage will be those against whom you've raged before.

When do you rage? In other words, what specific events trigger your rages? Some of these triggers may come from others, such as your partner mentioning that he or she wants to spend a few hours tonight away from you. But it's just as likely that the trigger event is something you think about all by yourself, such as the possibility that your partner might want to spend some time apart. You will probably quickly notice definite patterns here. For example, you may recognize that you can't stand it when your partner uses the phrase "I just need to have a little alone time" or when you think to yourself, "Why would anybody want to stay with me?" Eventually, you will need to find ways to neutralize these highly emotional words and thoughts. For now, though, just stick with the detective work.

How do you rage? What do you say? How do you act? What does your face look like? What happens to your voice? Do you swear? Do you hit, push, shove, or choke people? Rages are so overwhelming that you may not know everything you say and do during them, so you may need to ask other people for information here. If so, don't get too defensive ("No, I don't do that! I'd never do that!"). Instead, listen carefully to what others say.

Why do you rage? This is the biggest question but also the hardest to answer. The key is to go back to the moment you began raging and ask yourself this question: "What was happening right then that made me feel abandoned or betrayed?" Use this format:

When he/she said _____

I felt _____ *(abandoned, betrayed,…)*

Because _____.

Or *When I thought* _____

I felt _____ *(abandoned, betrayed,…)*

Because _____.

Here are two examples:

When Suzy mentioned a coworker told her she looked sexy, I felt threatened and scared because I thought she would want to get involved with him.

When I thought about how great Suzy looks with her new hairdo, I began to feel empty and vulnerable because I convinced myself she got her hair done to attract other men.

Do these rage-triggering thoughts make sense? No, of course not. In each case, the rager takes a neutral event and turns it into a relationship-threatening one. And that is probably exactly what you do when you have abandonment rages.

STEP 2. *Commit to quit raging, no matter how jealous, empty, lonely, hurt, insecure, or unsafe you feel.*

Irrational jealousy is a major problem for people who feel deeply insecure. They may find themselves looking through their partner's purses or wallets for any hints of infidelity. They make ridiculous accusations. They constantly demand proof that their partners love them and only them, when nobody can ever prove such a thing. No matter how often their partners reassure them, they feel so empty and desperate that they never feel safe. They worry and fret, because deep down inside, they do not feel like "keepers." They are just convinced that, sooner or later, their partners will come to their senses and leave them for a better person. That core insecurity can lead first to jealous doubt, then to foolish accusations, and finally to abandonment rage. You know full well, if you have problems with jealousy, that you are constantly tempted to follow, listen in, question, and accuse. Don't do it. Stop yourself.

There are moments of truth in any healing process. Some people call them "gut checks." You need all your courage, commitment, and conviction to get through these moments. You will find them occurring frequently when you try to quit raging about abandonment issues. That's because people in relationships continually face situations where the person they love and need leaves them for at least a brief period. Even your loved one running to the store for a newspaper or a pack of cigarettes may be enough to initiate an abandonment rage on a day when you are feeling particularly insecure. It may be very tempting, then, to start an argument just to keep him or her from going out the door.

Still, you have a choice, no matter how shaky you feel. You can keep screaming, yelling, whining, and badgering your partner, until he or she really does leave you, or you can make and keep a commitment to quit raging, no matter how unsafe you feel. That choice seems deceptively simple on paper, though. Who wouldn't want to choose not to rage when you have everything to lose if you keep raging? But you know, if you are an abandonment rager, you will be sorely tempted to keep exploding. Inevitably, your partner will say something that triggers your abandonment fears. Sooner or later, you will think something that increases your doubts about that person's love and loyalty. These tests will occur. But when they do, you cannot allow yourself to give in to your fears. You must remind yourself of what's really important in your life. You must keep your promise not to explode.

This promise is particularly important if you are a jealous person. You just cannot allow yourself any excuse to accuse or attack your partner. You must not give in to your jealousy, because if you do, that jealousy will ruin your life.

STEP 3. *Make your main goal to exchange the sense of distrust that fuels abandonment rages with a willingness to trust.*

One idea I've found really helpful as a therapist is the substitution principle. The idea is simple enough: whenever you want to quit one thing, you must always find a replacement for it. For example, you can't just say to yourself, "I should watch less television." That won't work unless you add "… and start reading a book" or doing something else that is interesting. Without substitution, if you just try to quit something without finding a replacement, you create a vacuum, a blank area in your life. That empty space will usually be filled once again by the very activity you are trying to stop. The substitution principle applies to thoughts as well as actions. You can't quit thinking one way until you've found a new approach.

Distrust is the fuel for abandonment rages. "He's going to cheat on me." "She's going to leave me." "They're going to let me down." "I can't trust anybody." These thoughts must be replaced, because they regularly trigger abandonment rages. The question is with what can you replace them? I believe the answer is with a willingness to trust. Now, that isn't an easy task, by any means. Your brain has been well trained to be suspicious and distrusting. Deciding to trust will feel like an uphill climb for quite a while. However, thinking in a more trusting manner gets easier the more you do it. Eventually, you'll reach the top of that hill and start coasting down.

How do these thoughts grab you?

- "Today I choose to trust [someone specific here]."

- "From now on, I'm going to trust [someone specific here]."

- "I'll give [him/her/them] the benefit of the doubt."

- "I want to be more trusting. I can be more trusting. I will be more trusting."

- "I am more trusting now than I used to be, and I will continue to develop trust."

- "My world is safer than it used to be. I've just got to accept that fact."

- "[Someone specific here] loves me and wants to stay with me."

I suggest you select a few of these thoughts to repeat frequently to yourself. Pick the thoughts that feel right. And come up with some of your own. They won't be ones that you say to yourself and then think, "Oh, sure, that's a bunch of bullshit." They will be ones that you say to yourself and then breathe a sigh of relief. They will help you feel safe in a safe world. Most importantly, those ideas will help prevent abandonment raging.

STEP 4. *To gain greater ability to trust in the present, focus upon people whom you have been able to trust in the past.*

If I asked you to tell me whom you've been able to trust in the past, how would you reply? A friend? Your sixth grade teacher? A past lover? One parent or stepparent? A brother or sister? A counselor or social worker? Those buddies from the gang you belonged to? A grandmother or an uncle? Hopefully, you've been able to trust several people during your lifetime. If not several, at least one or two people proved trustworthy. But what if you answered, "Nobody"? I wouldn't accept that. That's probably a personal myth you've created to validate your urge to rage. Everybody has found in their lives a few people they could trust, if only for brief periods.

Take some time now to think about those people who earned your trust. How did they do that? What did they say? What did they do? Did they keep their promises? Did they stick around, even when you tried to push them away? Did they believe in you, even when you could not? These people were trustworthy. They earned your trust, not just by being there once for you but by being there repeatedly. You could count on them, maybe not every time you needed them (they were only human), but often enough.

So what? How does the mere fact that some people were trustworthy some of the time heal the pain from other important people being untrustworthy all too often? Here's how. First, it shows you've had some good luck and shown good judgment in the past. You've found people you could trust. You'll be able to do so again. Second, these people have kept you from losing all hope in humankind. They've helped you believe that you can be loved, safe, and accepted. Third, and most important, they've shown you what to look for now and in the future. You can distinguish between people who make false promises and people who keep their pledges.

Trust is the key to preventing abandonment rage. But not blind trust. Not naïve trust. The trust you need is based on faith that you can find and keep people who really want to be loyal and true to you. They will be people a lot like the people you've been able to trust in the past.

STEP 5. *Replace jealous, suspicious, and distrusting words and actions with trusting ones.*

Trust is more than an attitude. It's also a collection of words you speak and actions you take. So, if you experience abandonment rages, you will almost certainly need to change your words and behaviors.

Perhaps before continuing, we should decide what trust is. Synonyms for the word "trust" include certainty, belief, faith, confidence, reliance, hope, and conviction. To trust someone, then, implies that you truly believe that person is on your side. If you believe this, you can feel far more secure in your relationship than. when you are full of doubt. You can feel confident in your partner's love and loyalty.

It is critically important, if you want to quit raging, to learn to speak and act in trusting ways. To see why, just take a look at how Bettina's habit of distrust affects what she says and does.

Here are some of Bettina's distrusting words: "Where were you? Who did you talk to? What did you talk about? Do you like her? How much? Do you like her more than me?" She predicts out loud that Mason will leave her, just like her past partners. She tells him that she is so needy, she knows Mason will get tired of trying to please her. Also, Bettina asks Mason over and over if he really loves her, but when he says yes, she tells him she doesn't believe him. And here are a few of her distrusting actions. She follows Mason to make sure he isn't seeing someone else. She calls other women to tell them to keep their hands off him. She constantly tries to read his mind, so she can accuse Mason of "thinking about" leaving her. She tries to get him to stay home every evening instead of going anywhere without her.

What are the results of all these distrusting words and deeds? As Bettina says, "I drive my partners away with my accusations, suspicions, and jealousy." But that's not all. She also keeps convincing herself that people cannot be trusted. So Bettina gets stuck in a terrible circle. Because she distrusts, she says and does things that drive people away, which only increases her distrust.

How, then, do you start trusting? First, by making a serious promise to yourself to trust others, especially your partner, more.

Remember that the habit of distrust you have developed is unhealthy and unneeded at this time in your life. Second, you must consistently give your partner the benefit of the doubt. That means no more accusations, endless questions, or demands for proof that he or she loves you. Each useless question only adds to your insecurity, no matter what answer you get, so quit asking. Third, police yourself to catch your fears and doubts before they can take over your mind. You will really help yourself if you can say, "Oh, oh, I'm getting paranoid again. I better stop thinking that way right now." Fourth, develop a trusting vocabulary. That means saying things like "I trust you" and "I can depend on you," both to yourself and out loud. Notice you're not saying "I wish I could trust you" or "I'd like to depend upon you." You're also not saying "I trust you, but…" which of course means you actually don't trust that person. Fifth, act in a trusting manner. In order to do this, ask yourself one simple question: "What would a trusting person do in this situation?" Then act that way, even if it doesn't feel natural.

STEP 6. *Learn how to accept reassurance when you need reminders that you are loved and wanted.*

Insecurity haunts people prone to abandonment rage. They keep asking themselves and their partners if their partners really love them. Unfortunately, their ears have been trained only to hear this: "Well, no, actually you can't trust me. I figure I'll leave you in a few months, but only after I've cheated on you and stolen all your money." Reassuring answers, such as "I love you more than anything. I want to stay with you the rest of my life. I promise to be true," seldom are heard. And if they do get through, they are met with an inner response like this: "Oh, sure, that's what you say. That's what they all say. I don't dare believe you." Those prone to abandonment rage have trouble believing anyone could love them for long. The fear of abandonment lingers like a late morning fog blocking out the sun. However, this particular kind of fog is mental. Instead of water droplets, the abandonment rager's fog is composed of little particles of suspicion, worthlessness, fear, and anger. This fog blocks out sunbeams of comfort and love.

So how, then, can you cut through the fog? You must get better at taking in the love and reassurance that others offer. That calls for conscious effort. For instance, take a deep breath every time your partner says he or she loves you. Take the words deep into your body. Breathe them into your heart. Hold onto those words until they get past the brain-doubt barrier and into your soul. Choose to believe that you are loved, appreciated, and accepted. Let the sunlight in.

It's okay to ask once in a while for reassurance. "Do you really love me?" is a normal question, at least at the beginning of a relationship. Just be sure to absorb the reassurances when they are offered. Don't stand there like a wooden stick when hugged. Instead, fold your arms around your partner and feel the warmth. When alone, remind yourself that you are loved. Keep a mental picture of your partner being loving toward you. Hear his or her words again. Feel the hug.

The fog of doubt won't dissolve easily. It might even break up for a while and then return. But don't get discouraged. You can learn to feel safer, much safer, by taking in your partner's reassurances. By shifting from relatively insecure to secure, you will also help yourself avoid abandonment rages. Why rage over feeling abandoned if instead you can feel connected and cherished?

STEP 7. *Challenge yourself to let go of especially painful feelings of neglect, abandonment, rejection, or betrayal from the past.*

Neglect: "My mother got hooked on drugs and quit taking care of us."

Abandonment: "I felt ripped apart when my parents divorced and my dad moved out. I still can't accept it."

Rejection: "My ma told me she wished I'd never been born."

Betrayal: "My parents promised me they'd never leave me. Then they dumped me on my grandmother and took off."

Neglect. Abandonment. Rejection. Betrayal. These are four types of injuries that pull people toward insecurity. Recent injuries like this are terribly painful. But the worst wounds are often the most ancient ones, those you received early in life. These hurts (including those that may have occurred when you were too young to consciously remember) shaped your beliefs about relationships. They formed filters for your experience that are still active today. What goes through these filters? Any evidence, however flimsy, that people will neglect, abandon, reject, and betray you. What gets filtered out? Any evidence, however powerful, that people will be loyal and loving toward you. The result is a distorted universe skewed toward doubt and distrust. No one can be trusted.

Imagine going through life with an endless stream of doom-predicting parenthetical thoughts like these:

- "He says he wants to take care of me (but he'll start drinking and drugging just like Mom did, and then I'll end up taking care of him)."

- "She's offered to move in with me (so then she can tear me apart when she leaves, just like when Dad and Mom divorced)."

- "He says he accepts me completely (but that's bullshit, since he'll end up wishing I was never born, just like Ma did)."

- "She says she'll never leave me (which is just what my parents said before they dumped me on Grandma)."

You rage to keep people from leaving. You rage to protest past and future abandonment. You believe that, sooner or later, every important person in your life will neglect, abandon, reject, or betray you. You've got to quit thinking that way if you want to stop raging. The six steps described above will certainly help you think in a more trusting manner. However, there is one more step—a big one—left. You need to challenge those demons from the past, those early attachment injuries. You have to leave the past in the past, once and for all, so that your present becomes uncontaminated.

You must accomplish this cleansing of the soul in your own way. Here are several approaches that might help you get free from the past.

Believe that you are not doomed to repeat the past. You have the ability to create a new world in which you are surrounded by loving, caring, and loyal people. Besides, you need to believe in a good world in order to expel the bitterness inside you that fuels your raging.

Remind yourself every day that the people in your life today are not the same as those in the past. This is an essential task. Your wife is not a younger version of your mother. She is a completely different person. Your boyfriend is not a clone of your father, even if they both went prematurely bald. Your kids aren't miniature versions of your brothers and sisters. They have their own personalities.

Keep a journal. Journaling can be very useful if you write about a past attachment injury, allow yourself to feel your pain and anger, and then write about how that event happened long ago and how you can let go of it. You can also use the journal to help you notice the differences between your past and current experiences.

Consider therapy with an experienced counselor to help you deal with these issues in a safe and supportive atmosphere.

Talk with people you already trust about your desire to be more trusting. Tell them that you want to learn how to trust people more, especially those people who have earned your trust.

Forgive those people who neglected, abandoned, rejected, or betrayed you in the past. This will help you recall times when those same people were kind, caring, and loving toward you. That will, in turn, help you realize that people are not totally good or totally bad. And that recognition will help you accept the most important people in your life today, so that you won't rage at them if they occasionally fail to appreciate you.

Religious or spiritual study could help you let go of everything you cannot control, including what happened in the past. It could also help you replace feelings of bitterness with a more positive sense of gratitude and serenity.

Abandonment rage is a killer. Don't let it destroy you and the people you love.

The Bottom Line: A Life
Free from Rage

Willy's Success Story

When Willy, forty, began seeing me for counseling a couple of years ago, the first thing he said was, "My wife Penny has moved out. I want her back. Can you help me?" You can probably guess why Penny departed. Willy was a sudden rager who had never really tried to stop. But his wife's action served as a wake-up call. Willy truly loved her. He was eager to do anything to reclaim her affection, up to and including working on his anger issues.

Now, just being strongly motivated isn't enough to quit raging, of course, but it sure helps. In fact, even before he saw me, Willy had said "no, thanks" several times to rage opportunities. But he had also said "well, yeah, I think I will rage, thank you very much" a few times as well. The last time that happened was when he asked Penny if she was coming back to their home soon. She didn't answer right away. Here's Willy's description of what happened:

"I tried to stay calm. I told myself to be patient. But I only wanted one answer. And when she didn't say right away she was coming home, I just lost it. I could feel myself changing, but I couldn't stop. I didn't really want to stop. My rage came out, and I screamed at her. I accused her of wanting to sleep around. I called her every name I could think of. I don't even remember everything I said. The next day, she served me with divorce papers. She said it was that last rage that made up her mind. That's when I decided I needed help."

Two years later, Willy and Penny have reconciled. I met with them both. Here's Penny's report: "Willy doesn't rage anymore. He still gets angry, sometimes over stupid stuff. But even then, he stays pretty calm. We can talk now, and he actually hears what I say. Sometimes, he has to take a time-out if he's getting too mad, but then he comes back and we figure things out together. It took a while, but most of the time now, I feel safe with him."

Willy works hard at preventing raging. He's learned to recognize early cues that he's getting in trouble, even though at first he swore that his rages came completely out of the blue. He takes antidepressant medication, because he discovered that his untreated depression greatly affected his mood and made him more likely to rage. He uses thought-changing exercises to help him challenge paranoid thinking. He exercises. He's cut back on caffeine and completely quit drinking alcohol "because I need to stay in control of my brain." He's also discussed some important family-of-origin issues in therapy that help him understand why he could treat Penny disrespectfully. Willy is also quite humble. He knows that the minute he thinks he'll never rage again will be the start for his next rage. So he tries to learn everything he can about anger management and rage prevention.

Still, when I ask Willy what's the secret of his success, he goes back to the issues of motivation and belief in himself: "I told myself I could stop raging. I made myself stop raging. I finally decided that I deserved to have a decent life."

A Review of the Concept of Rage

We've covered a lot of territory in this book. So let's end with a review of the main ideas.

Rage is an experience of excessive anger. Rage is an event triggered when you have too much anger to handle normally. Basically, raging represents an emergency alternative to how you usually deal with anger. When talking with the person you're upset with goes nowhere, when "stuffing" your anger doesn't work, when taking a time-out is useless, when thinking about a problem just makes you crazy, when nobody understands, when relaxation is impossible, when everything the frontal lobes of your brain suggest fails—that's when you are ready to rage.

Rage is a transformative experience. Something changes inside you during a rage. The measure of that transformation is one or more of these three possibilities: you lose conscious awareness of what you say and do; you feel like you are a different person in a kind of Dr. Jekyll and Mr. Hyde temporary personality switch; you lose control of your behavior, saying and doing things that normally you would and could control.

For every total rage, you probably have several partial rages. Not all rages are consuming events. Many are smaller mini-rages, in which you only lose partial control. You need to learn everything you can about these partial rages to maximize self-control.

You may often have near-rage episodes as well. These are times when you come very close to a meltdown, but somehow you stop. Here too, you need to study these events. Perhaps by doing so, you can discover the small but critical differences between almost having a rage and actually raging.

Not all rages look alike. One big division is between sudden and seething rages. While sudden rages occur very quickly and often with little warning, seething rages build over days, weeks, months, and years. If sudden rages are like tornadoes, then seething rages are like underground fires slowly burning up everything in their paths.

Another way to divide rages is by the threat that each rage addresses.   Survival rages defend against a perceived life-threatening physical assault. Impotent rages battle a deep sense of being unable to control important aspects of your life. Shame-based rages try to annihilate anyone who has intentionally or unintentionally shamed you. Abandonment rages are out-of-control protests against the threat of someone leaving.

If you are a rager, you aren't the only one in the world with this problem.   Probably up to 20 percent of the population has had at least occasional rage episodes. Most of these rage events are partial rages. Nevertheless, raging is always dangerous and can be fatal.

Rages can be prevented.   Rage prevention is the name of the game. It is the key to a better life. Frequently, you can stop a rage before it happens if you take a time-out or use other standard anger management techniques. You may also want to try certain medications that keep your brain from having a meltdown.

Each kind of rage needs to be treated a little differently.   The six chapters in this book detailing different types of rage each have their own set of suggestions for change. You will need to study these ideas very carefully. You may also figure out other good ways that help you handle your rages. Please remember that you don't have to do this alone. You may need to recruit family, friends, professional counselors and doctors, spiritual advisors, and others in the very worthy cause of helping you quit raging.

Here's the bottom line: Raging can be stopped. You can quit raging. You can have a better life.

References

Amen, D. 1998. *Firestorms in the Brain.* Fairfield, CA: Mindworks Press.

Bowlby, J. 1969. *Attachment.* Vol. 1 of *Attachment and Loss.* New York: Basic Books.

———. 1973. *Separation: Anxiety and Anger.* Vol. 2 of *Attachment and Loss.* New York: Basic Books.

———. 1980. *Loss: Sadness and Depression.* Vol. 3 of *Attachment and Loss.* New York: Basic Books.

Feeney, J., P. Noller, and M. Hanrahan. 1994. Assessing adult attachment. In *Attachment in Adults,* edited by M. Sperling and W. Berman. New York: Guilford Press.

Freedman, S. 1999. A voice of forgiveness: One incest survivor's experience of forgiving her father. *Journal of Family Psychotherapy* 10(4): 37–60.

Green, R. 1998. *The Explosive Child.* New York: HarperCollins.

Karen, R. 2001. *The Forgiving Self.* New York: Doubleday.

Kaufman, G. 1996. *The Psychology of Shame*. 2nd ed. New York: Springer.

LeDoux, J. 1996. *The Emotional Brain*. New York: Touchstone.

———. 2002. *Synaptic Self*. New York: Viking.

Neihoff, D. 1998. *The Biology of Violence*. New York: Free Press.

Newman, K. 2004. *Rampage: The Social Roots of School Shootings*. New York: Basic Books.

Papalos, D., and J. Papalos. 1999. *The Bipolar Child*. New York: Random House.

Potter-Efron, R. 2001. *Stop the Anger Now*. Oakland, CA: New Harbinger Publications.

Ratey, J., and C. Johnson. 1998. *Shadow Syndromes*. New York: Bantam Books.

Slevin, P. 2005. Suicide note is confession to slayings. *New York Times*, March 11, 11A.

Ronald T. Potter-Efron, MSW, Ph.D., is a psychotherapist in private practice in Eau Claire, WI, who specializes in anger management, mental health counseling, and the treatment of addictions. He is the author of *Angry All the Time* and *Stop the Anger Now*, and coauthor of *Letting Go of Anger, Letting Go of Shame,* and *The Handbook of Anger Management.*